MISS PEGGY LEE

Miss
Peggy
Lee

BLOOMSBURY

First published in Great Britain 1990
Copyright © Peggy Lee 1989

Bloomsbury Publishing Ltd, 2 Soho Square, London W1V 5DE

A CIP catalogue record for this book is
available from the British Library
ISBN 0 7475 0470 9

10 9 8 7 6 5 4 3 2 1

Grateful acknowledgement is made to Jerry Leiber and Mike Stoller for the
right to reprint the lyrics from 'Is That All There Is?'. © 1966, 1969, Jerry
Leiber Music & Mike Stoller Music.

Grateful acknowledgement is extended to Johnny Mandel for the right to
reprint 'The Shining Sea'. Lyrics by Peggy Lee, music by Johnny Mandel.

Photoset by Rowland Phototypesetting Ltd,
Bury St Edmunds, Suffolk
Printed and bound in Great Britain by
Butler and Tanner Ltd, Frome and London

'Louis Armstrong said I always knew how to swing . . . I just seem to understand about swinging – I always did.'

In the same intimate voice, and with the same winning directness with which she delivers her haunting songs, Peggy Lee now tells her remarkable life story. It's as if she were just sitting across the table.

Norma Egstrom was born in 1920 in North Dakota and her mother died while she was still young. Her stepmother abused her and at fourteen she was running her father's railway depot while he got drunk. Only when she left her home town did her prospects improve; singing for Benny Goodman in 1941 was the turning point.

So the story of Peggy Lee emerges, touring with the Goodman band; through several stormy marriages; frequent battles with terrible illnesses; the Oscar nomination for her performance in *Pete Kelly's Blues*; her autobiographical Broadway musical *Peg*; her courageous stand in legal problems ranging from a lawsuit involving Lassie's daughter to a 3-million-dollar suit over her great hit song 'Mañana'. And then there are the wonderful stories behind the songs – 'Fever', 'Lover', 'Johnny Guitar', 'Black Coffee', 'I'm a Woman' – the roll-call is dazzling. She wrote over 200 lyrics herself and recorded over sixty chart-busting albums. Her friends are all here too – Frank Sinatra, Bing Crosby, Nat King Cole, Paul McCartney and many, many more.

It is a life just as brave and swinging as her fans all over the world would expect of her.

Dedicated to my daughter,
Nicki Lee Foster,
and my grandchildren, David,
Holly and Michael

With love,
Mama Peggy

CONTENTS

The Family Tree

I changed my name legally to Peggy Lee but when I began to write this autobiography, I was overwhelmed by the number of names involved before I was even born.

On my father's side, let's start with John Erickson, who was born on a farm near Stockholm, Sweden. I had always been told that Norwegians and Swedes didn't get along together; however, John met and married Bertha G. Olson in Arndal, Norway. I had also been told I was three-quarters Norwegian and one-quarter Swedish, but let's just say I am Scandinavian.

John left for the United States. Crossing the ocean, he was shipwrecked. John and five other sailors made a raft and for thirty days they floated on the ocean. Four of them died. A ship picked up the remaining two men and they were taken to Bellevue Hospital in New York. John had a six-month loss of memory and after his release he refused to sail again. I should think not!

He finally remembered Bertha and wrote to her in the old country. Her parents thought he had deserted her. He did not know that by then he had a son, Eric Emil Erickson. It took seven years before John had enough money to bring the family over to New York. Bertha's sister accompanied her and Eric to the United States.

The second son, Ole, was born in New York. He was my Daddy, Marvin Olaf Egstrom (Erickson). Later, when they all got their citizenship, Marvin kept one family name, Egstrom, while the others all remained Erickson after John. Ole had three other brothers, Eric Emil, Edward and Julius.

On my mother's side, Oleana Johannsdatter was born in Toten, Norway, on 14 September 1879. She married A. L. Anderson in Redwing, Minnesota, and became quite a famous milliner. She made grand hats of ostrich plumes and velvet with fine tulle and malines. (She left a huge box of ostrich plumes dyed all different

I

colours and beautiful velvets and veiling.) People would drive hundreds of miles by horse and buggy to buy Grandmother's hats, which sold for fifty dollars and up. According to the 1897 Sears and Roebuck catalogue, less fashionable hats sold for two and three dollars. Untrimmed, they sold for as little as fifty cents.

Grandmother must have been one of the first liberated women. When she died in 1922, the headline in the Volga papers read: 'Business Woman Passes Away'.

(My sister Della made a gown for me from a bolt of Grandmother's malines. It was so fragile and beautiful, and she sewed it all by hand. Years later, when I began my career as a professional singer, I wore this same gown, but when the spotlight hit it, the malines disintegrated and fell in pieces, and I was left standing in my slip.)

Oleana and A. L. Anderson had two daughters: Josephine Mathilde and Selma Emele. Selma was born on 13 February 1885. Selma Anderson and Marvin Egstrom met and fell in love. They eloped to Volga, South Dakota, when Selma was sixteen years old. Her mother, Oleana Anderson, was such a strict disciplinarian that Selma was afraid to tell her she had eloped. 'Either you tell her or I will,' Marvin said.

When Grandmother Anderson heard the news she was shocked for a moment, but then she said, 'Well, if you're old enough to get married, you're old enough to run your home properly.' So she put Mama in a finishing school, and I'm glad she did. Looking back on these family histories, I have grown a little bit fond of Oleana and suspect that my own home is run properly because of the example set by my mother.

Selma Emele Anderson and Marvin Olaf Egstrom had seven children: Milford, Della, Leonard, Marianne, Clair, Norma and Jean. Gloria was still-born.

Selma loved her father. He had lived with the Indians and from them had learned how to filter water through charcoal. He invented the first charcoal filter which bore his name – the Anderson Charcoal Water Filter. (In later years his son Leonard persuaded him to sign over to him the patents for the water filter. It's my understanding that he drank the profits away.)

Grandfather Anderson was fascinated by the notion of perpetual motion and kept pursuing it until he went blind, after which my mother brought him to live at our house in Jamestown, North Dakota. I loved to listen to his stories of the Indians and of people

like Wild Bill Hickok and Calamity Jane. When Mother became ill
– she fell into a coma – Grandfather was sent to a home and stayed
there until he died.

I was born Norma Deloris Egstrom on 26 May 1920 in Jamestown,
North Dakota, and I'm still growing up.

Prologue

'Is that all there is?
Is that all there is?
If that's all there is, my friend
Then let's keep dancing,
Let's break out the booze and have a ball,
If that's all there is . . .'

I picked up the needle from the demo record on the turntable and said to Snooky Young, 'Isn't that wonderful?'

'That's a weird song,' he said. 'You going to sing that?'

'Yes, I think so. I can't get it off my mind.'

'Well, you do all those kind of arty songs and people seem to love them . . .'

I thought of 'Don't Smoke in Bed' and a few others and remembered how I often had to fight to get to do things I believed in, but little did I know at the time what a battle I'd have with 'Is That All There Is?' Before this, its authors, Jerry Leiber and Mike Stoller, had written 'I'm a Woman', truly my cup of tea, and, of course, their huge success, Elvis Presley's record of 'You Ain't Nothing But a Hound Dog' (although I still think 'I'm a Woman' was more colourful, filled as it was with word-pictures, and it did swing).

When I came to record 'Is That All There Is?' there was resistance everywhere. They said it was too far out, they said it was too long, they said and they said . . . So I went to Glenn Wallichs with a demo record (something I hadn't done before), and Glenn seemed embarrassed. 'Peggy, you don't have to play a demo, you helped build this Capitol Tower. You just record anything you want.'

Delighted to hear it, Jerry and Mike and I set about doing just that. Earlier, Johnny Mandel had brought me one of Randy Newman's very first albums, telling me, 'You'll love this fellow,' which I did, and I asked him to write the arrangement. It turned out to be perfect for his style.

So now the record was made, our faith in it ran high – I couldn't believe my ears when Capitol Records said they were turning thumbs down on it.

Is that all there is?

No, because, fortunately, there was a television show they wanted me to do, which I wasn't too keen about. Well, you know what I did. I said, 'Yes, if you'll release this record, I'll do the show,' and they agreed.

Hallelujah. It became a hit, went 'across the board', but that's not all there is to it. It dramatized for me what my life had been and would continue to be, a struggle, sometimes for things more serious than a song, but the lesson was there – stick to your guns, believe, and more than you ever imagined can happen!

1

Norma Deloris Egstrom

I was four and I was watching my mama in a hospital bed, but the bed was in the parlour. There was a nurse walking quietly outside the door in soft white shoes. I saw my mother weakly get out of bed and try to drink the water out of the flower vases. Some of it spilled on the floor. Poor Mama, she was *so* thirsty. They took her flowers away.

The scene changed and the bed was gone. Instead, there was a coffin and in it lay my mama, sleeping so peacefully, looking so tiny and beautiful. People stood around with sad faces, and the ladies were all wearing hats.

I broke the booming silence: 'Can I see my mama?'

Wordlessly, they placed a straight chair by the coffin and lifted me up. A Scandinavian lady standing in the group behind me whispered loudly, '*Ven* are dey going to make coffee?'

Then they closed the lid and gently carried her out the door.

'Where did they take Mama?'

'To heaven with God.'

'Where's God?'

'Up there.'

Now the days all ran together. I was a strange child. I had been alone a lot while Mama was in a coma for all of those months. The quiet came naturally, and my dog and I watched everyone go about their business with wide eyes enquiring. I became curious about nature. Leaves, flowers, little rocks – sometimes I'd turn them over to see what was growing underneath. Strange to remember one little rock after all those years. It had something to do with Mama. Someone said they had put her in the ground and someone else said she was 'up there'. So I'd lie on my back and look up at those big white thunderclouds we used to have in North Dakota and I was sure that one day Mama would peek out from behind those clouds.

Somehow that felt so good – just thinking she was near – but when the wind blew the clouds away, I was left with the same old question: where did they take Mama?

Well, maybe one day I'll know.

The first time I saw Min, the lady who was to be my stepmother, she was dangling a ball of candy on a rubber string. She had a gold tooth. She was smiling, but I could tell she wasn't smiling at all. It was as if I knew what was going to happen. Children are like that.

Florid face, bulging thyroid eyes, long black hair to her waist pulled back in a bun, heavy breathing, German descent – wore cotton dresses from Sears and Roebuck or Montgomery Ward. (During the Depression they used to call their catalogues 'wish books', for obvious reasons.) She read *True Romances, True Story* and similar magazines; ate chocolates – lots of chocolate-covered cherries and Whitman Samplers, drove the Model-A Ford like it was a Ferrari.

Obese and strong as a horse, she beat everyone into fright. Even the men were afraid of her. She would trick people into a corner and attack their most sensitive spots. When others who didn't know her were around, she would talk in a sickeningly sweet way.

That first day I stood in front of her shyly, with my hands behind my back, wanting very much to have one of those jawbreakers, covered with little specks of candy. I think it took about a week to eat each one.

'Look what I bought for you,' she puffed. I finally gave in and reached for the ball of candy.

Somehow I knew then they were soon to be married. It was a year after my mama's death. Min had been my sister Della's nurse when little Paul was born. Mother had died in August and now it was two days after Christmas. That night there was a blizzard so Daddy built a roaring fire. We had gone to bed. I was sitting on the bed in my daddy's room when Milford came running in.

'Dad, the house is on fire!'

'Naaaaw, you go to bed.'

'No! Put your hand on the floor, you'll see!'

Daddy swung his feet over the side of the bed and discovered why Milford was standing on one foot and then another. He put his hand on the floor and felt the heat! In a state of shock he put on one layer of clothing after another. Poor Daddy! I think the things that had been happening, one after another, were just too much for him.

Milford was running around rousing Leonard and Clair and Marianne. You could hear them shouting.

'Leonard, where are my pants?'

'To hell with your pants. I've lost my sock!'

Poor bewildered Marianne just sat there until she was ordered out of the room, carrying her clothes under her arm.

We all went outside into the cold, whistling blizzard; Marianne was in her nightie, and I guess that's what I was wearing too. They moved my sister, Della, out of the house with the newborn baby, bed and all. It was thirty-five degrees below zero and snowing.

Marianne and I watched like it was a ping pong game: the firemen ran in and out of the house, throwing furniture on the lawn and soaking it with water (thereby invalidating the insurance, it turned out).

'I kept asking, 'Where's Jeanie Finkbinder?' (one of my play-mates), but either they didn't hear me or they weren't much interested in my questions. The flames were crackling and the smoke blended with the whistling snow. I suppose the fire kept us warm, but a coat would have helped.

We stayed overnight at the Finkbinders' house, but all we could smell was smoke, so the next day we were sent to the Lipperts' house. They were Min's ex-in-laws. Her husband had blown his head off by sticking it into a big gasoline tank and lighting the match. I wonder if he did it on purpose.

Sometimes we would stay with the Schaumbergs, who were Min's parents. They had a nice house and they were good to me. Grandpa Schaumberg would sit in a big oak rocking chair by a Boston fern with his meerschaum pipe. Near him a giant clock tolled the hour and ticked loudly while he read his newspaper that had been sent to him from Germany.

Sometimes I would watch him peel potatoes: he would peel the whole potato the thinnest I ever saw without breaking the skin and it would come out the other end of his paring knife like a spiral. He always bought green bananas from some refrigerated freight car. I don't remember ever eating a ripe one – I wonder who did?

Every afternoon I was told to go into the parlour and take a nap – that is one way to get rid of a little kid. In the parlour, wonder of wonders, there was a player piano, which I would pump as hard as I could down on my hands and knees. Sometimes they would make me stop and I would lie there and count the buttons on the leather couch.

I would get lonesome for Daddy and would go out and sit by the iron picket fence – waiting and waiting for Daddy to come. He very seldom did. But I still remember one day sitting there plucking grass and trying to make it whistle, as I had seen some bigger kids do. I put the blade between my thumbs and blew on it – once in a while, I would get a little whistle. Then I saw some pointed yellow shoes and I looked all the way from the pointed toes, up to the knees, up the clothes and there was Daddy smiling down at me. When I finished squealing with delight, he told me he had come to take me to dinner at a café.

We had hot-roast-beef sandwiches with gravy all over. It's funny, I don't remember any other time my Daddy took me to dinner. But that was certainly a great hot-roast-beef sandwich . . .

Summertime in North Dakota could be wonderful, especially if you were anywhere near the James River and you went on a picnic where the trees hugged the river banks and the river broke up the flatness of the land.

I remember the park where my brother Clair and I were sent out with gallon syrup pails to pick gooseberries. I would fill up my pail as quick as I could because afterwards we were allowed to go swimming. Clair would talk me into trading buckets: 'Here, Hoot-chie, I'll trade you buckets,' and I would. Then when I went to empty his bucket at Lipperts' I would find he had stuffed the bottom with grass and leaves. I was so embarrassed because it looked like I was trying to cheat. (As much as he loved me, Clair loved to outsmart me.) They would send me back to pick more gooseberries, and Clair would go swimming.

When it was watermelon weather, we children ate watermelon and marched around the block with the rinds on a long stick. We also played king of the hill, hopscotch, and I was always careful not to 'step on a crack, you'll break your mother's back'. I don't know why stepping on a crack bothered me so much when I knew my mother was gone, but they had said she was 'up there' and I suppose I just wanted to know she was all right.

When there were thunderstorms at night, I was petrified. I was told that if you were near feathers, you would not get struck by lightning, so I walked around with a pillow all night long, feeling fairly safe.

We moved to 215 Milwaukee Street East, and there were few of the comforts of home. Nights went by when Daddy didn't come home until very late. I was afraid, not knowing where he had gone, but sometimes I would finally fall asleep with my head on my arms on the dining-room table.

Once in a while, I would have a toothache, but as soon as Daddy put his warm hand on my cheek, it would disappear and I'd go to sleep so fast you wouldn't believe it.

Sometimes I followed Daddy to work. If he saw me, he would stick his first finger out, and I would grab it, and he would take me to the depot with him, me trotting as fast as I could to keep up with his giant steps. He would put me up on a big stool, give me some paper and rubber stamps and I would stamp away very nicely until he could find a way to get me home.

(I remember there was a little boy at the depot who told me where some jelly beans were kept in the warehouse. We would sneak in, take handfuls of jelly beans and tiptoe out the back and eat to our heart's content.)

One day Daddy didn't see me running behind him. He must have been in a hurry and suddenly he turned a corner and he was gone. I sat down on the sidewalk and began to cry. A lady gave me some toys to play with and said, 'Don't worry, your Daddy will be here to pick you up.' I remember being puzzled at how Daddy knew where I was. I guess I decided daddies just knew everything. A telephone call was the answer, but I had never heard of a telephone.

The day after Daddy and Min married, he hadn't been out the door five minutes before she laid down all the ground rules.

I had done the unforgivable. In a strange house, terribly lonesome for my mama and missing my daddy, I wandered into their nuptial chamber crying, 'Mama, Mama.'

Well, the battle lines were drawn for the next eleven years. 'Norma, you go out there and cut yourself a willow switch, and don't try to cut a little one, because if it breaks, you'll have to cut another one!' Her florid face flashed in front of me as the switch cut into my skin. After she had vented her anger, she made a little speech about my not bothering my father and that if I told him, there would be 'more where that came from'.

All the kindness was gone. Where were the tender smiles and happy laughter, with rustling taffeta, the sound of crystal, the feel of fresh linen and the smell of flowers? It seemed like yesterday Mama was still there, making lovely delicate things for us, baking delicious cakes and cookies, singing and laughing, playing games with us, playing her prize possession, a Circassian walnut piano. And then she was gone, and there was this great heaviness and the anxiety of impending evil.

Although I was only five years old, my work had begun. Min would have me stand on a box and wash dishes. If the water was not hot enough, she would pour boiling water over my hands. I began to be terrified of what each new day would bring. What was life all about? Did this happen to everybody? Was I any different? I'd wonder why my daddy was my daddy. I loved him, and I am glad he was my daddy, but why couldn't I have belonged to the Zellers down the street? I heard them talking about adopting me, but my daddy wouldn't have liked that. I was his favourite, perhaps because I was the youngest.

One very hot day we had a rip-roaring North Dakota thunderstorm. It cooled the air and everything seemed so beautifully fresh and clean, smelled marvellous. I went out to join the other children in the neighbourhood, wading in the puddles. But I slipped and fell in the mud. Within minutes Marianne and I were being soundly whipped. For her grand finale, Min broke the skin on our backs. We ran upstairs and listened through the furnace register. Min and Daddy were talking about 'the books' again . . .

I often wondered why Daddy and Min got married. Was it because of what Marianne and I heard through the register about Daddy being asked by Mr Stebbins to 'fix up the books a little for the good of the railroad'? It was something about the *per diem* reports. Was it because Daddy was drinking and Min knew and might tell on him?

I didn't want to imagine him loving her after Mama.

First grade was the only bright spot. I loved school and our wonderful teacher Ella Fetcher. She had to scold me in front of the class, though, when I got my first 100 mark – I put my paper in my mouth while pretending to be looking for something in my desk. 'You can put your paper away now, Norma. Everyone has seen your 100 mark,' she said. I blushed red as a beet.

Miss Fetcher would draw a birthday cake on the blackboard whenever it was someone's birthday. She would say, 'What kind of frosting do you want?' and then she would draw all kinds of coloured roses and flowers and put the candles on it. 'Blow out the candles and make a wish,' she would say, and you would pucker up to blow. As you did that, she would take the eraser and wipe the yellow flames from the candles – you would always get your wish because you always blew out all the candles.

Jamestown was an exciting place, with the big railroad stations for the Great Northern, the Northern Pacific, the Sioux Line and, of course, the Midland Continental Railroad that was 100 miles long and held them all together. The railroad was the only way of connecting the miles and miles of flat prairie and transporting the freight cars, refrigerated cars and flat cars to all those far off places. (One time the refrigerator car broke down, and we had oranges for ever! When you lived on the prairie in those years, an orange was a magical, exotic fruit – you might even eat the skin and smell the scent of the oil in the orange peel.)

The Midland Continental Railroad was founded and funded by a wealthy widow who intended it to run from the Canadian border to Florida but ran out of money after 100 miles. It was built by an English engineer who named each town after one in England. It always sounded so grand to me when the conductor announced that the Midland Continental would be stopping at Jamestown, Wimbledon and Edgeley.

The railroad had on its tracks not only a great steam engine, but also a truck and a Model-A Ford on railroad wheels, which they would use to deliver the mail or take the cream cans in to the dairy.

The train would stop wherever people were waiting along the track. They counted on the railroad to take them to the nearest doctor or to pick up some mail or baggage. Most had no other way of reaching a destination. There were very few passengers actually riding on the train. One day I hung a roll of toilet paper off the end of the caboose, and as the train rolled, it unravelled. I always did like flags. Mr Kellogg, the conductor, and Mr Simmons, the engineer, were good to me, and besides, who was going to see? Mr Simmons once let me blow the big old whistle and I'll never forget the surge of power I felt when that big blast came out. I jutted my chin out just the way Mr Simmons did. He laughed so hard and tried to put his striped cap on my head but it fell down over my nose.

But now we were leaving Jamestown for Nortonville, and the most dreadful part of my life began.

Daddy had been demoted to the little station in Nortonville, which I think just about broke his heart. I don't think the railroad approved of the marriage. It was in the middle of the Depression. Nortonville was a tiny town surrounded by farms with about 125 people trying to survive and make some sense out of life, usually failing, or so it seemed. Daddy looked very sad and began to drink a little more. As late as two in the morning, I'd find him down at the depot singing and talking to the railroad tracks with a Ralph somebody.

Marianne, Clair and I seldom found much happiness. I remember helping Marianne gather her clothes and hiding them out behind the barn so she could run away to live with our older sister Della and her husband and little Paul. I was severely beaten but I refused to tell where she had gone. We had undergone a number of beatings together and a closeness had developed between us that would never be broken.

My brother Clair would try to make me laugh, but mostly the joke was on me – he was always talking me into milking the cows in exchange for 'helping with the dishes', but he had always disappeared when it was time for his end of the bargain.

By now Min had opened up her whole bag of tricks. She would hit me over the head with a cast iron skillet and beat me with a heavy leather razor strap with a metal end. It made a scar on one side of my face that even now tries to show up in a photograph. It didn't matter to her what her tool of torture was; she used anything that was handy – and she loved to drag me around by the hair. I was always covered with gouges from her nails, which she dug into my arms or wherever she grabbed me. The mental cruelties were another story. She was constantly saying my head was too small for my body and my hands were too big. I was just all wrong. She would also say, 'You will come home with a big belly,' but I had no idea what she meant.

My teacher, Mr Earl Clark, used to try to help. When he saw me running down the road he would ring the school bell until I reached the safety of the school yard so I wouldn't get a tardy mark and be punished for being late. He really was kind to me, and I have always been grateful.

Later I helped Clair get away. He tried to persuade me to come along but I couldn't leave Daddy with her. I had to stay there.

By the age of seven I was keeping house. By ten, I was baking large batches of homemade bread, milking cows, churning butter, cooking and cleaning. The following year I had my first paid job, taking care of a newborn baby and the mother, plus the farm animals, cooking, cleaning, milking cows, washing clothes with water I carried from the creek. (The family was so poor they didn't even have a well.) The whole area was so primitive there was no electricity, no indoor plumbing; inside there were kerosene lamps, Benjamin Franklin stoves, wood-burning ranges, and no music, unless I sang. I was paid two dollars a week, no days off.

Everybody has to be someplace, I guess.

When bringing the cows in for milking, the bull was to be kept separate and was supposed to stay behind in the pasture. Well, I watched him out of the corner of my eye while I brought the cows out one day and *he* was watching *me*. I was fumbling with the harness used as a makeshift closing for the barbed wire fence. The barbed wire was a little taut, especially if you were as scared as I was with the bull steadily approaching – eye to eye now. With one last desperate tug to slip the harness through the rings, it suddenly acted like a big slingshot and hit me right in the eye. I went out like a light.

When I came to, I heard some very heavy breathing. I cautiously opened my eyes to see two large nostrils sniffing at me. Nose to nose we were.

After I realized he wasn't going to eat me, I wasn't afraid of him any more, and he lost interest in me. I *was* glad to go home in the fall, however, even if Min was there.

At about this time I met Everold Jordan, known to me as Ebbie, who was to be my best friend. Whenever he could, Ebbie would come and help me with the heavy chores, and in turn I would help him shock grain, pitch hay, or whatever was to be done at the Jordan home.

He knew about Min, but we didn't talk about it. He just tried to help me and make me laugh. After we had done our chores, we would drink Rawleigh's Mouthwash together, thinking we were

terribly sophisticated, as we stanchioned the cows in the warm barn.
We used to take turns telling each other our one joke – the only one
we knew: there was a man who got his nose cut off and his toe cut
off; they put his nose back on where his toe should be, and they
put his toe back on where his nose should be. And after that, every
time he had to blow his nose, he'd have to take off his shoe.

Then we'd laugh and laugh. I still do when I think of it.

One day in 1927 I saw the smoke coming out of the chimney at the
town hall. I knew it meant something special was happening there
– the smoke in the chimney was the signal. Anything would have
been special in our little town of Nortonville, but this was really
something special! I ran down to see what it was.

It turned out to be a double feature. Two movies! Ginger Rogers
in *The Thirteenth Chair* and Al Jolson in *The Jazz Singer*. Oh, I
could hardly breathe. A real movie. A travelling show. (Little did
I know that one day I would sing duets with Al Jolson on his radio
programme and that I would co-star with Danny Thomas in *The
Jazz Singer*.)

The town hall wasn't even a theatre, it was just a hall where they
held everything: basketball games, box socials, dances where Clyde
Moller and his family would play. One of the Mollers chorded on
the piano while Clyde played the valve trombone. They would play
'You Are My Lucky Star' and the dancers would stand there and
pump their arms up and down before they took that first step. You
could almost guess how good they'd be by how long they pumped.
It was even exciting to go outside and hear the music coming through
the walls. A few of the men had half pints of home brew and they
tipped their heads back and guzzled. Mysterious and sophisticated,
I thought them. They probably didn't know there was a child
watching them.

I was so excited I can only remember part of the movies – Ginger
Rogers must have been a child then, and she looked so beautiful.
Al Jolson was singing 'Sonny Boy' in blackface, and I was crying
my eyes out. It's hard to believe that down the road a bit I would
have the honour of meeting Miss Rogers and in my own dressing
room.

There were no street names or numbers on the houses in Nortonville.
You would just refer to the name of the family who lived there –

the Conitz house or the Hollingsworth place. You would go up the 'sandy road' from 'downtown' or the depot to the Egstrom house.

One day I was going down the sandy road with two dozen eggs to trade in for sugar, singing at the top of my lungs. But the sand was pulling at my ankles and it knocked me over – on top of the eggs. I sat there for a long while and tried to figure out how I would tell Min. 'Uh, I was walking down the, uh.' No, that wouldn't do. 'A big wind came up when I was walking down the, uh.' No, that was a lie. She'd never believe that. 'Well, the bag slipped out of – ' How could it do that? I was hanging on to it for dear life! I guessed · I'd just have to blurt it out and take my lumps.

It was 1929, the stock-market had crashed, and we began to see men crawling down the sides of the train and rolling out from the rods under the cars. The train men just ignored them; they knew who they were. The stockyards, down a way from the depot at Nortonville, became the hobos' hotel. The railroad ties and heavy boards used for construction were a weathered grey – not very inviting – but down there, semi-protected from the elements, were the hobos who rode the rails during those Depression years. When the train stopped, the 'bo's' would hop off and find a little place to make a campfire. Sometimes they could steal an egg or two from a chicken or take the whole chicken, for that matter.

There was one traveller who really shook me up. He was wearing burlap wrapped around his feet for shoes. Poor man! And he really needed to see a dentist. I can never forget watching that egg slide over his broken teeth.

Full of compassion for these fellows, I used to tell them where we lived up the road so they could come and get a free meal. They did. They came up and asked for work, like chopping wood or hauling in coal. Oh, my Lord, I felt sorry for these men. They came from all walks of life and had just been mawled nearly to death by the Depression. They could barely manage a smile but they surely let me know they appreciated the trust from this strange little girl.

Somehow, my daddy found out about my breadline. He nearly went berserk. It was one of the few times he scolded me, because he was afraid of what they might do. But they didn't do anything but good. They chopped the wood I would have had to chop and did all kinds of other jobs. I appreciated it and they would say,

'Thank you, Ma'am, God bless you,' as they went on their way. Probably wouldn't be that way nowadays with drugs and all, but those poor souls needed a friend.

Sometimes Min went to Jamestown, which meant she was away all day and maybe part of the night. My sister Della had sent me an embroidered silk cloche hat – pale peachy pink. I never was allowed to wear anything given to me. It was always kept for something 'good', but there was never anything good. With Min away, I put on my hat and went over to Ebbie Jordan's house.

Out in the barn we played hide and seek. I crawled up the manger post to where canvas binders were stored, tied up like tarpaulin. Terrific! If I climbed on top of that, I could watch Ebbie go crazy looking for me. I had barely got out there when the whole thing gave way and dropped me. My forehead was so badly scraped I never thought to look for my hat. I combed my bangs to hide the scrapes but Ebbie looked at me and sang, 'One-two-three for Norma!'

It became a habit of mine to slap my forehead whenever there was the slightest breeze to make sure my bangs were plastered down. Until my forehead healed, I lived in fear that Min would say, 'What happened to your hat? What happened to your forehead?' Luckily, she never found out.

When I was ten I was very ill. The waves of nausea and the retching kept me up all night long, then I fell into some kind of delirium. I remember seeing my brother Clair standing at the end of my bed. 'What's the matter, Hootchie?' he was saying, and I couldn't even answer him. I had ripped my nightie while I was writhing around. I guess I was trying to get out of the pain. He had been to look for Min, who was showing her nice side to the Ladies' Aid Society. Somehow he managed to get her to come home. I'm quite sure she hoped I would not pull through. As a nurse she should have known the symptoms, known I had appendicitis (and by that time, my appendix had burst and peritonitis had set in).

Clair hadn't gone to school that morning. He was frightened enough to fight Min. Somewhere he had picked up a double-barrelled shotgun, and the next thing I remember was Clair telling her with cold anger that she'd better get me to a doctor.

'How am I going to do that? There's no doctor around here.'

'Yes, there is. In Edgeley. Get moving. You're not going to let her lay there and die. You move or I'll shoot you.'

He pulled one trigger and then the other. Thank God, both barrels were empty.

Dimly it comes back that they put me in the car and drove me eighteen miles on a rough gravel road to Edgeley and Dr Green. In those days, that took about four hours. I don't remember much about the ride . . .

The 'hospital' was over a small bank – three or four rooms and the operating room. The whole place smelled of ether. There were some fairly primitive surgical tools in glass cabinets and the operating table was black leather. There was one nurse but she was a patient too, and there was another doctor besides Dr Green. I heard him moaning in another room. Someone said he was 'taking a cure'.

They laid me down on the black table and put me to sleep with ether. As I was going to sleep, I could hear flapping sounds, first at one end of the room and then at the other. That was my first encounter with ether, and I didn't like it at all.

When I came to, I wanted water so badly . . . I couldn't find any, and there was no nurse to bring it to me, so I got up and looked for it – and that saved my life. Walking was good for me, although I didn't know it at the time.

Each day I would walk to the window and stare at an enormous tumour they had removed from some woman. They had placed it in a pan and put it out on the roof of the next building. It started out as large as a small watermelon, and the last time I saw it, it was like a small cantaloupe. I guess they had forgotten where they put it.

Then, finally, came the day to go home. I took the train – Edgeley was at one end of the Midland Continental Railroad. I guess I hoped someone would be glad to see me, but Min was there, as frightening as ever. I had been gone for ten days, but the only thing she had missed was my work. Straight away she told me to scrub the floor. I was so weak I could barely carry the bucket and scrub brush, and I was so dizzy that I could hardly see the floor. But I was afraid not to try.

My abdomen was bandaged and had drain tubes for the perito-nitis. But that didn't stop her. I honestly think she was frustrated that I had survived. Suddenly, she started kicking me in the stomach, and she just kept kicking until she broke open the incision.

I cowered behind the wood-burning range until it was safe for me to come out. Then I found some bandages and tape and did my best to put myself back together.

When I saw Dr Green the next time, he was horrified. I didn't tell him who did it, but he said he knew. He patched me together and sent me home again because there wasn't anything else he could do.

This was a little more than I could stand and I told Daddy. He tried to protect me, but then she beat him. It was blizzarding outside. I grabbed my overshoes but only got one on – the other was on the porch – and I was running. Daddy followed me, yelling, 'Run!' Min was after him with the poker. We got away from her and Daddy took me to our neighbours, the Bucholtzes. They were as terrified of her as everyone else and stuck knives in the door jamb so she couldn't get in. They told me later they thought they saw the handle of a butcher's knife stuck in her overcoat pocket.

After two or three days Min went to the depot and begged Daddy to bring me back. Of course, she wanted me back, there was housework to be done. She convinced Daddy that she would never touch me again. I was very reluctant to go back with him. I didn't believe her, and I was right. Only a day went by before she was at it again. It got so that if someone walked by me I would flinch. I always felt sure she was trying to kill me, and I would run around to the side of the house and sit and hug my little dog, who was shaking with fear. I think the love that came from that little dog may have helped me go on . . .

And I remembered Mama. One day when I was sitting in the attic looking at pictures of her, Min found me and the photos of our whole family. She burned them all, but she couldn't burn my memories.

Nortonville was full of characters. There was a man named Fred Bitz. Thin and wiry, he was a small man with black eyes and his face all drawn up towards the centre. I used to see him every few days when he would come in to the depot with his cream can; we would weigh it and pay him for it and he'd be off to get himself a drink. He was a quiet man, didn't seem to take up much space. One day he came in, got his cheque and then we didn't see him again. Not until a day when I was out in the bean field in the August sun – the temperature gets to be around 105° or 110° at that time of the year. You could see the heat waves rising from the ground. Hopping down the row, I raised my head to wipe the perspiration from my forehead and saw something shimmering through the ragweed at the edge of the bean field.

Ebbie Jordan was with me helping me pick the beans. 'What's that green thing in there?' I asked him.

'I don't know. Looks like a car. Let's go see.'

As we approached, Ebbie said, 'Looks like Fred Bitz' car. What's it doing there?'

'I sure don't know. Yes – it *is* his car. Model-A Ford. What's that smell?'

'Oh, my God. Who's in that car?'

We looked in, and there was Fred. We figured he'd been there since that last cream cheque. Blue flies were buzzing and maggots crawling.

We ran! There wasn't any law to call. We just told anybody we found and brought them back.

It seemed he'd rigged up the exhaust pipe to the front seat. Or did he? It remained a mystery. His brother-in-law sold moonshine and the last people to see him were the folks at his house. After they buried him, some folks wanted to dig him up again for an autopsy, but his brother-in-law didn't want that. No one ever really knew what happened, but they certainly wondered.

And then there was Hoover – a little six-year-old boy who seemed to be going on three. Hoover was fascinated by one particular duck that sat in our pond. Most any time you could find him down there with a bucket trying to drain the pond. If you asked him, 'What are you doing, Hoover?' he would answer, 'I'm going to get that duck.'

My ambitions lay in a different direction. The ad said, 'If you sell two dozen cans of Cloverleaf Salve, we'll give you coupons toward a diamond watch.' And, of course, there were a lot of lesser prizes, but I said, 'That diamond watch! I'll get that diamond watch!' Let Hoover have his duck. I wrote in for the first two dozen cans of Cloverleaf Salve, which had all kinds of good things in it, like carbolic acid and vaseline.

The excitement of that salve arriving! I *never* got a package before. I couldn't even imagine how it could find it's way to me.

I sold salve 'till the cows came home', and every time I sold two dozen cans, I was sure I'd get the watch, but I didn't. They would just say, 'Now you've almost sold enough salve' – yes, you've guessed it – 'to get the diamond watch, or more Cloverleaf Salve.'

I was so enterprising I should have had a manager. There was some horseradish growing near the artesian well. I nearly broke my back digging it up, then I ground it in the meat grinder, tears rolling down my cheeks, added a little vinegar, and sold it for ten cents a quart.

Ebbie and I teamed up as business partners, but I'm a little ashamed of one venture. We made radish sandwiches and seasoned them with a little chicken manure for our imaginary restaurant customer, Hoover. Hoover never knew why we snickered as he ate them.

Ebbie and I used to ride around on an old plough horse named Beans. There was plenty of room for both of us, but one day a little boy – I think his name was Robbie McClelland – asked Ebbie if he could ride with him. Ebbie said, 'No, not today, Robbie.' He smiled back at us, gently slapped old Beans with the bridle rein and rode off. The horse stepped into a gopher hole, pitched forward, throwing Ebbie off, and then crushed him.

Ebbie's family mourned him deeply. I did too. I loved Ebbie very much.

Springtime was my favourite – still is – with crocuses in bloom after the snow melted and pussywillows standing there so straight with those soft little buds all up and down. One day in May when I was about seven, I went down to Bone Hill Creek. No one was around, not a soul. The creek was swollen with spring water, and the Civilian Conservation Corps had built a dam to hold it all there. It was a great place to swim.

I couldn't see any reason why I shouldn't be able to swim the way the other people did. Everyone could swim, couldn't they, if they just tried? So I stripped down to my panties and started to wade into the creek. It had a mud bottom, and as I walked out into the deeper water, I began to lose my balance. Now I was getting frightened, trying to walk on my toes, but there wasn't anything to walk on.

For a second I dared to look over my shoulder, and suddenly the shore was a lot farther than I thought. Somehow, with all my wiggling, I had left the shore behind, and even though the creek wasn't terribly wide, I was too far out – too near the middle. Where was the bottom? The water came up to my mouth, and I had to swallow some. Then, panicky as I was, I started to dog paddle and, thank the Lord, I managed to get to the other side. I walked back down the creek to a narrow spot where there were rocks so I could cross over and get my clothes, and decided to try a swimming lesson another day with someone there.

The following year, when I was eight, I went to Spiritwood Lake; it was the only vacation I'd ever had, so you can imagine how memorable it was. I saw a drunk passed out in the hot summer sun with flies crawling around on him and immediately thought of Fred Bitz – except this body was breathing. Another little girl was standing looking at the drunk, and for the lack of anything else to say, I announced, 'I'm going to be in show business someday.' She was impressed and said, 'Oh yeah? What are you going to do?' I said, 'Sing, like this,' and broke into a chorus of 'Here comes the showboat, here comes the showboat, shuff, shuff, shuff, shuff, shufflin' along . . .'

I didn't even *know* that girl, yet she believed me, and that helped me believe it, too.

Spiritwood Lake must have been named after the legend: whenever there was thunder and lightning, two logs were said to come up in the middle of the lake and bob around together. They were the Indian girl and her lover who had drowned out there together because their folks wouldn't let them get married. I *saw* the logs . . .

I used to get up before dawn and take the fishing pail, the bait and the pole and get in the rowboat and row out, the oars kalunking along, and catch perch and pike and a few shiners too, but you threw those back.

Back at the pavilion, I cleaned the fish and helped them clean up the kitchen, peeled potatoes – whatever they wanted. When Rudy Vallee was singing on the radio, I was in seventh heaven.

Well, they said I was so good, they were going to hire me for eight dollars a week next summer. You bet I'd take the job. But the next summer they didn't call me for the job, after I had spent all the money I would have earned in my mind, picking out school clothes and presents for anyone I could think of out of the catalogues. I learned that one about not counting your chickens before they're hatched. It still was the best summer I ever had, though. At Spiritwood I learned to swim very well. I swam a mile behind a boat and dived off the high tower – twice, in fact. The man said he'd give me a whole quarter if I'd dive off the high tower; when I did, he said he didn't see me and made me do it again! Of course, he did see me. How could he miss me with the belly whopper splash I made both times?

Back home in Nortonville, I was going to show off again when we drove down to the Civilian Conservation Corps dam. I just ran out on that board to spring up and do a lovely swan dive – only the water had drained way down, and I went head-first into the mud, feet sticking up. The water had been ten feet deep and now it was only up to my knees. So I got it again – don't count your chickens, and don't show off.

Way out behind the little town of Nortonville there were the mounds. I'd found them while I was looking for arrowheads and tomahawks. Someone had told me they were Indian graves and from that day I knew I was on sacred ground and tried to behave that way.

It was a strange, quiet place that filled me with a deep feeling of sadness; I would sit there on the ground and cry. I wondered if those arrowheads had been part of the battle that killed the Indians who were buried there. With a child's imagination I saw them in their head-dresses silently stalking. After I was scared enough, I'd run home, but somehow I felt I knew those Indians, perhaps because of my grandfather Anderson and his stories of the Indians.

During the Depression we moved from the house up the sandy road to upstairs over the depot. Times were really tough. I remember expressions like 'Easy on the butter, kids, it's fifty cents a pound,' although we had our own butter from our cows, old Billy and Sally.

On Sundays, after I had milked the cows, separated the milk, washed the separator and put a pot roast in the oven, I always liked to go to church early so I could play the piano. It was probably the only one in Nortonville at that time. I'd play 'Out of the ivory palaces, into a world of woe . . .' until someone came in, and I'd stop.

One Sunday after the services were over I was walking back over the field to the depot. I looked up and saw smoke billowing out of the windows! I ran as fast as I could across that field and around the side of the depot where the door to our living space was.

Min was lying on the ground. She had slipped on some ice by the pump and couldn't get up. Her leg was broken right in two. She was in a lot of pain, but it was a good thing she had slipped, otherwise she would have been up the stairs trying to put the fire out when the gasoline stove exploded. There wasn't anything I could do but run for help, which I did.

I felt sorry for her, but we were not exactly sad that she had to go to the hospital for about eight weeks. People sent things from all over the state, including a pair of ladies' shoes with high heels and pointed toes, which I wore with rubber bands around them to hold them on. When Min came home from the hospital, she cut off the heels and made me wear them to school. They turned up at the toes and the other kids laughed.

I never dared tell anyone except Ebbie about Min's cruelty. Once I told another friend, but she told her mother and I got another beating for telling.

Oh, what a loving dog Rex was. I named him Rex because even though he was a mixed breed, he was king to me. He was a silver-grey and his eyes were amber and full of adoration – adoration for me but not for the pack of hounds who were his mortal enemies. They got him one day and ripped him from one end to the other. He managed to drag himself home, and I cried so hard I could hardly see him.

I did manage to carry him upstairs and make a bed for him. Then I cleaned his wounds and tried to get him to drink some water. The poor dear couldn't even raise his head, but he feebly wagged his tail to let me know he appreciated my love.

He died that night and I sadly carried him down by the railroad bridge. The ground was frozen, so I covered him with an old khaki army blanket and put stones around him so the wind wouldn't whip the blanket away.

Many times during the winter I went to visit him there and in the spring I buried him.

After milking the cows in the morning, there was laundry to be done. I used to scrub the shirt collars and cuffs with Fels Naptha Soap until my knuckles were bleeding, then put them into the hand-operated washing machine. I thought that everyone lived this way, in the grey chill of impending violence. One of the cruellest things Min did was to make me butcher the animals I had named and thought of as pets – the chickens I had scooped up in my arms and brought in out of the rain.

One morning when the frozen suits of underwear filled the washing lines like stiffs and my stepmother had driven into Jamestown, I walked quite calmly to the medicine chest, took a bottle with a skull and crossbones and poured out a glass. I had just put it to my lips when my stepbrother came in, having forgotten something. It startled me enough to pour the stuff into the sink. He went back to the car and never knew what I was attempting to do. Being about eight or nine years old, I didn't have the wisdom to know how good life could be.

You may well ask, 'Where was your Daddy?' Well, he was probably out trying to drown his sorrows, and, besides, I tried to hide everything from him; he was so troubled.

'I'll leave when I find out where these railroad tracks lead,' I used to think.

In 1934 we moved to Wimbledon, a slightly larger town. The railroad had transferred Min to Millarton, where she spent most of her time. Daddy took advantage of that, and I was left to run the station while he drank far too much.

The Midland Continental Railroad ended there in Wimbledon. You could go to Jamestown, Nortonville, Edgeley or some other smaller places, but this was the end of the track. In my mind's eye, I couldn't see any further, and I still wonder where those cars went. I had a fierce pride in that railroad and when I got a little older, if I ever heard someone make a derogatory remark about it, I would take advantage of my position as editor of the high-school paper in Wimbledon to write a scathing editorial.

Across the street was the depot for the Milwaukee line, where we used to exchange waybills. I can still see my daddy walking from our depot to theirs, waybills in hand, hat cocked at a jaunty angle. No matter where Daddy went, he wore a three-piece suit, neatly shined shoes, a clean shirt and a hat now and then. It strikes me as being a little sad that he would get all dressed up for a tiny town like that. Perhaps in his own mind he was still superintendent of transportation or, at least, station agent . . .

Why should I have been embarrassed if he'd have a little too much to drink and do an Irish jig in the post office? He wasn't even

Irish, but you'd sure think so with his singing and dancing. It's OK, Daddy. Sing me an Irish song!

When the train came in, I'd be so glad to see Mr Kellogg, the conductor. He used to let me take some hard coal from the train to make it easier to start the fires in the depot – especially in the winter, when we had mostly lignite. I'd have to lug in approximately a ton of lignite to bank four different stoves throughout the night. I had to stoke the stoves and replenish the fire sometime in the day or usually night. What a job. I learned to lift with my thighs, and learned about leverage, which comes in handy once in a while.

We had to melt snow for water for bathing and washing. I'd put a copper boiler about three feet long and three feet deep up on the range, then go out with a shovel and cut a big square of snow to fill the boiler. I made it into a game. The trick was to see how big a square of snow you could carry into the kitchen without it breaking all over the floor. Even if it broke, though, you could sweep it out the door and have a nice clean floor for your trouble. The hardest part was to get the boiler full of water down off the stove. That was usually accomplished by smiling slyly at some unsuspecting man who came by.

The part I liked best about running the station was that Daddy was around even though he was drinking. He was fun.

At least once a year we'd have a big snowstorm and the train would get stuck or even snowed under. One of the train men would crawl out and hook the telephone wire on the train to the regular telephone line. In the depot we had one telephone on the wall with a handle to grind, but the one on the desk had a carbon cone for a speaker, and you could always hear the conversations all along the line on the 'company' phone . . . 'Well! We're snowed under all right. When do you think those snow ploughs can get out here?' 'Oh, I don't know, depends on how much they have to plough through.' 'OK then, but bring us some food out here. We'll probably be here a while.' 'How about some Baby Ruth bars and some Snickers?' 'Yeah, we could use some of those too.'

I used to listen and picture all this going on, and somehow it sounded so cosy. Cosy, my eye, I'm sure they would have said.

There was one train a day, unless they sent out a 'special'. Those other lines – the Milwaukee, the Northern Pacific, the Sioux Line, the Great Northern, even the Santa Fe – kept us busy transferring from one line to another.

Even at fourteen I didn't do too badly at running the depot. One time, though, I made a pretty big mistake. There were two junk men who were always competing to see who could get the most scrap iron out of there, and they had to book the loading platform in advance. Well, not realizing how long it would take them, or even that it was important to them, I reserved the loading platform for both of them at the same time! If I hadn't been so young, I don't know what they would have done to me.

I used to hear remarks from people like, 'They'll be sending that back in bullets' and 'That will all be coming back to us.' It sounded important, and it was, but I didn't understand. This was 1934. It took only seven years – to December 7, 1941 – for this scrap to become the stuff of war.

Wimbledon in 1934 seemed like it was full of cobwebs. The railroad station was old, the hotel across the street was old and deserted; a family lived there – a mother and father and a little girl named Helen – but there were almost never any guests. Except once.

Helen was my playmate. We had a big galvanized wash-tub down in the basement, and during the hot summer we sat in that tub for hours on end, or at least until the sun went down.

I can still see that hotel. There was a check-in desk and a big book to register names and a bell to tap for a bellboy, except there weren't any. Behind the front desk there were boxes for the keys and the mail, in case there ever was any mail. There was even a dining room, and on the second floor were rooms, but only two beds had mattresses. The lobby had a great wide picture window in front so you could see who was inside. There were a couple of rocking chairs and a big brass spittoon between them. I used to think I saw an old man sitting there rocking, but I guess I didn't. Anyway, he wasn't there when Helen's folks left on a trip and I got my father's permission to stay overnight with her.

When we heard the bell ring at the desk downstairs, we nearly jumped out of our skins. We ran down, and there were two men asking for rooms. What a thrill to finally have someone come to the hotel! We really played our parts, welcoming them like royal guests. Of course, we had to explain that we just had the one room available. They didn't mind, they said. They were so tired they'd just take anything. They seemed a little reluctant to sign the register, but I guess they thought, what the hey, we might as well humour the little brats.

We asked if they would like something to eat, and, yes, they would. Again we had to apologize, we only had egg sandwiches, but you can't go too far wrong with those, and we were soon serving them in the dining room. We never expected to have so much fun.

After they finished eating, they were anxious to get some rest because they said they really had to get going in the morning. So we ushered them to their room, wished them a good rest, and tried to calm ourselves down as we washed the dishes and put everything in order.

Helen said no one *ever* stayed there. Maybe business was catching on? Maybe we'd have more people? What would we feed them? I could go across the street to the depot and get a little something for their breakfast . . . We babbled on until we wore ourselves out and went to bed from sheer exhaustion.

When we woke up they had left without paying, but that ceased to matter when we found out they were two fugitives wanted for murder! They had picked the perfect place to hide.

Up on Main Street there was a candy store, a café, a general store, a post office and a milliner's shop.

It was so eerie, that shop. There was a small bay window with a couple of dusty hats sitting in it. No lock on the door. I'll never forget how Helen and I tiptoed in that first time. All the furniture was still there, and the wind blew old letters and papers back and forth across the room. We went into the kitchen, and all the pots and pans were still on the stove with the old dried-up food in them.

And then we learned the whole family had died of diphtheria, except the widow, and she just high-tailed it out of there. From wherever she had gone to, she always paid all the taxes so no one could touch the building, even though everyone said it was an eyesore.

Any time you wanted to feel spooky, you could just go in there.

Another big attraction in Wimbledon was the wonderful souvenir Harry Hanson had brought from Hollywood, where he used to be a 'prop' man. Everyone used to go and see it many times and marvel over the fragile beauty of it, me included.

He said it was Janet Gaynor's brassière!

It was really a lovely bra – and I enjoyed the fantasy, too.

2

Miss Peggy Lee

'How can it be so hard to get away from nothing?' I thought as I looked out the window, looking at the flatness, while absentmindedly washing a plate, and I thought, 'Yes, I *am* going to be a singer. I *know* it.' It was just a matter of fact. It was as if a nice friend had come and whispered this comforting thought in my ear. No matter what happened afterward, I always remembered that moment.

I went around singing, 'I Never Had a Chance' – a song of unrequited love that I had yet to experience, but it was fun to pretend. I learned 'Moonglow' and 'In My Solitude' and other songs. What a glorious feeling to put myself in those moods, whatever they were, and know I could convince someone it had really happened to me.

Ivar Knapp was either the superintendent or the principal of our school. I don't remember which, but he was an authority figure. I wanted to sing so badly, I found it difficult to believe he would give me permission – but he did! Under a stern exterior, there was a heart of gold. We made a deal that if I got my homework in ahead of time, I could go to Valley City and sing with Doc Haines and his orchestra. I'd met Doc when he'd once played Wimbledon. It seemed everyone in Wimbledon always knew I was going to go *someplace*, and someone pointed me out to Doc and said, 'That's our little Hollywood girl, you ought to use her.' Doc was dark and handsome, and I even liked his glasses. He was also a college student, which made him seem really glamorous and sophisticated. You can bet I applied myself, including working for the National Youth Association to the tune of twelve dollars a month for washing blackboards and halls.

Mr Knapp kept his word, and I kept mine, so off I went, hitchhiking to Valley City to sing with Doc Haines, which led to a sponsored radio programme on Radio Station Valley City. How did I get so lucky? My sponsor was a restaurant, a college hang out, and they paid me five dollars, plus all I could eat. But I was so self-conscious – I remember trying to eat a butterscotch ice-cream sundae and act really sophisticated. It took me years before I'd order another one of those again. (Artie Carney told me later that he had the same trouble with butterscotch. Loved it but just couldn't handle it.)

When we were booked out on some little one-nighter, we'd get there somehow but sometimes the audience didn't. Once we started out in a blizzard. Our trailer loaded with all the instruments had a newly painted sign shaped like a rainbow on the side that read DOC HAINES AND HIS ORCHESTRA. We were riding along so proud of that sign when all of a sudden the trailer started swaying in the snow and pulling the Overland Buick back and forth with it. The Buick was heavy enough to hold with the tyre chains, but the trailer slid and flipped over in the ditch. We had been laughing, but we stopped right then.

The fellows all piled out and gathered together the instruments that had spilled in the ditch. The other car with us had to go back to Valley City and borrow Mrs Norgaard's clothesline to tie the big bass on top of the Buick. Then we all piled in and set off again.

By now the storm had picked up, and it was hard to see where we were going. At one point we stopped in a hurry because we heard a train whistle over the wind and the sound of the rolling cars. It was a good thing we did. There was a long freight train, which we couldn't see . . . We would have ploughed right into it. The engineer must have known that road was there and blew the whistle just in case.

Well, we finally arrived, and there were about three couples standing there waiting to dance. I sang 'Moonglow' through my megaphone, and they could hear a little bit of it, if they danced near enough.

Doc gave me fifty cents for the night, but I knew he was hungry, so I bought us both a bowl of chili with crackers. I had a crush on Doc. He used to call me his 'little blues singer'.

One summer I worked on a farm at harvest time. I cooked for the threshing crew for Mr and Mrs Ferd Flohr.

I never got over how hard Mrs Flohr worked, and I should know, because we worked side by side. First we had to get the cows in and milk them (no long fingernails in those days). I don't know how I found them that early in the morning, but they used to moo at me through the darkness as they headed in towards the barn with their udders heavy with milk. I'd have to get them in the barn, milk them and separate the cream from the milk in the big McCormick-Deering separator. Then I'd run into the house with the fresh cream and milk and pop the biscuits in the oven, get the oatmeal ready, fry up some bacon and eggs; maybe give the men a little fresh rhubarb sauce or some honey for the biscuits – and coffee and tea.

After breakfast there was canning to be done, peaches and pears and sometimes tomatoes to put up in Mason jars, place them carefully into the big copper boiler (as if we needed any more heat). While they were cooking away, it was time to clean the house, scrub the kitchen – sometimes wash clothes, but, glory be, Mrs Flohr had a Maytag washer which would putt-putt all those clothes clean.

One noontime the men were finishing their lunch, and I was rushing around in my overalls and hobtoed shoes (which I wore to save my good clothes). I had cooked a huge pot of stewed chicken and dumplings for dinner and was taking it down in the cellar to cool until it was dinnertime. It was a little dark going down there, and I couldn't see over the pot. I slipped and fell all the way down, the chicken and dumplings going everywhere. I landed in the coal bin – a drumstick here, a wing there, and gravy all over me, including my hair.

I picked myself up, felt for bruises and hobbled up the steps. Mrs Flohr and the men were laughing so hard you could say they might have split their sides.

Mrs Flohr was always laughing at me, but I didn't mind – I liked making her laugh; she had so little happiness in her life and was so nice, not anything like Min. I felt sad she never seemed to do anything but work. I didn't do anything else either, but I was used to it.

You know, Mrs Flohr treasured green grass so much that you had to walk a different way every time you went to any of the outbuildings, so you wouldn't make a path.

When I heard she died of cancer, I cried not so much because she died, but because she hardly ever had any fun. At least I had my singing. One time I was allowed a few hours off to go to an amateur contest. I sang 'The Glory of Love' and 'Twilight on the Trail' and won five dollars. It was just enough to pay for gasoline and beer for my brother, but I was so proud. I had won. I *sang* and they *liked* it. It still echoes down the years:

You've got to give a little,
Take a little,
And let your poor heart break a little,
That's the story of – that's the glory of – love.

Back to school, which was always fun for me. I was pretty good, except in a few subjects like home economics. I chose the most difficult thing to sew out of the most difficult fabric – a silk pongée brassière. Not because I wanted to show off, but because I wanted a silk brassière. (Later, when I was married, I tried to make a sheer black négligé, without a pattern, and wound up with a dozen sheer black potholders.) Reading directions is very important, yes, indeed. My brassière was held up to the class to show what *not* to do.

I got along fine with my classmates and my teachers. I always remember a poem written, I think, by my classmate George Brenner, who's at least a physicist by now:

> He who sitteth upon a pin
> may not see the point, but
> he will get it in the end.

For years I thought that the wittiest saying, but it's like the Katzenjammer Kids. For years I never liked them at all, but I would read them religiously every Sunday, until one day I revolted. I put the paper down and declared, 'I don't have to read them any more.' That was that, and I didn't. I was beginning to free my own mind . . . Some of us just go along believing what we read in the papers, in a book or a magazine, until that marvellous day people stop intimidating us – or should I say – we refuse to let them intimidate us, and we think and do things on our own.

The teen years went by so fast . . . I had ping-pong photos taken in a little booth like everybody else and hoped some unknown lover would want one. They were terrible – the photos, that is. I don't remember any lovers – just friends like the Joos brothers. One of the Joos brothers used to ride by the depot on a horse and the other, who played the trumpet and had the most beautiful eyelashes I ever had seen, went to Valley City College.

By the time I was fifteen I was singing at KOVC in Valley City; suddenly, all the fellows I saw were particularly good looking, but

I wouldn't let them know it, not on your life! They would look in the studio windows, and I felt like Clara Bow, the 'It' girl.

The summer I was washing dishes in a restaurant in Jamestown, I met Red Homuth: red curly hair, blue eyes, freckles and a great smile. He was the best-looking thing I'd seen, and he was an older man – well, he was the captain of the football team. He liked me. I liked him. One night when I was very anxious to see my dad, Red offered to drive me to Wimbledon to see him.

We arrived in Wimbledon going at a pretty good clip in his mother's car. The world was getting better all the time . . . I rarely saw Min now, which was the best thing that could happen, and now here I was, going someplace with my *boyfriend*.

Daddy was so glad to see me. He cast a sidelong glance at Red, but he seemed to like him – I think he knew it wasn't serious. It began getting dark; Red had to get up very early in the morning for his job driving the truck for the Nash Coffee Company, so he dropped hints about getting on, and we finally started back to Jamestown.

I said to Red, 'Let me drive. I *did* learn, you know, and you can get some sleep.'

Red hedged a bit, and then said, 'Well, I don't know about that. This is my mother's car, you know. Are you sure you can handle it?'

'Sure I can. It's practically straight all the way and probably no cars.'

'OK, Norma, you're on,' he said as he stopped the car. I jumped out and ran around the car with the gravel crunching around my shoes. It certainly got dark in a hurry out there. As far as you could see, there wasn't a light or a thing in sight. Dark, dark, flat prairie.

After an embarrassing jerky start, we got underway, and as soon as Red felt safe that I could drive, he leaned his handsome red curly head back on the seat and went to sleep.

I don't know how familiar you are with livestock signs in the country. From out of nowhere, not necessarily at a crossroad, in fact probably not, a sign will suddenly appear with the message: 'Warning. Livestock Crossing. Cattle Crossing. Watch for horses'. In the pitch dark, what does that mean? Before I had time to ponder, a herd of horses came out of the ditch right in front of us. I think I saw eyes glowing, but I'm sure I've never heard such a clatter and bang and crash as I did then. One horse went right over the top of the car; a couple crashed into the front and off the sides, hooves flying. The fenders wound up somewhere behind the car, the headlights were now out, of course, and the awful crunch we heard was the engine being shoved up between us in the front seat. Other things dropped off the car, one by one. Then there was an unearthly silence.

Finally, I said, 'Well . . . I guess I'd better squeeze out of here and see what I did.'

Red heaved a big sigh. 'Don't bother. I don't have to get out to know what you've done.'

It was hard to believe that neither of us was hurt, but somehow our budding romance wilted as we waited and waited for a car to come by. We just shoved the car in the ditch; I didn't envy Red trying to explain that to his mother.

I didn't see Red for a long time after that, but school went on. The halls were scrubbed, the blackboards were washed, I kept the depot clean, helped Daddy and hitch-hiked to Valley City to sing on the programme at KOVC. I also had the lead with Carl Erickson in the high school play. We thought we were wonderful, but I'm not so sure anymore.

I did well at graduation, but I couldn't *wait* to get out in the world, so I kissed Daddy, took my meagre belongings, and left for Jamestown again and my first very own residence. It was the corner of a basement, with a bed and an orange crate, but it was clean and safe. The only problem was knowing when to get up for my new job as relief girl in the Gladstone Hotel Coffee Shop. In the darkness of the basement, I could have slept my life away, until the people who owned the house gave me an alarm clock.

The excitement at the hotel . . . the heat and bustle of the kitchen, the flour rolls that would come sliding out of the hot ovens, the big chef Tony barking orders. I ran in and out of the kitchen acting like I was a real waitress.

That's where I met Bill Sawyer. He had been with the Cleveland Indians for a while, but now they'd farmed him out to the Fargo-Moorehead Twins. Bill was the first big brother in the outside world I ever had. He was the opposite of a wolf. He was the nicest guy and gave me all sorts of wonderful advice. He eventually became a professor at Western Reserve University.

He heard me sing in the KRMC radio station in Jamestown, which happened to be in the Gladstone Hotel. My accompanist was a minister's daughter who played pretty good jazz. When the team came in for coffee, they would tease me. Bill must have felt sorry for me, because he came over to the counter and said, 'Would it be all right with you if I wrote you a letter?' It was the first time anybody had ever asked me for my permission to do anything. I thought it was very nice of him, and the letter turned out to be full of really good advice – what books to read, be careful about going out with strange men . . . things that an older brother would tell his sister.

Bill also arranged an audition for me at WDAY, the biggest station in Fargo, and then drove me there – nearly a hundred miles (a long trip at that time). I was nervous about going with a comparative stranger, and having to stay overnight, but it turned out to be perfectly proper. We stayed in separate rooms at the hotel.

The following day he took me to the radio station. Out in the waiting room I could see Ken Kennedy, the head man, through the glass door. He was tall with reddish hair, blue eyes and a dimple in his chin. Bill had to literally shove me in the door. I was just standing there, rigid. 'Come on, Norma,' he said. 'You've come all this way. You're going in there.'

This was my big chance. Ken Kennedy brought in a pianist, I sang 'These Foolish Things' and he put me on the air that afternoon.

'You have to change your name,' he said. 'Norma Egstrom doesn't sound right. Ladies and gentlemen, Miss Norma Egstrom. No, won't do at all. Let me see. You look like a Peggy. Peggy Lynn. No – Peggy Lee. That's it! Ladies and gentlemen, Miss Peggy Lee.'

I was dizzy with excitement. I sang and they liked it!

Back in Jamestown I said a brief, sad farewell to all my new friends, including the gruff old chef, who held me on his lap and said, 'Yah . . . I knew our girl vud make it big. You don't forget and stay like you are, so schweet und nize.'

When I arrived in Fargo I thought it was the biggest city in the world. The main street was called Broadway and I walked up and down it, to the end called Lower Broadway. There I saw a sign that read 'Hotel – Vacancy – $2 and Up'. That was really more than I could afford, but I decided to try it for a few days. I walked up a flight of steps to the desk in the lobby. The clerk was not smiling.

'May I please have a room?'

'No vacancy.'

'But your sign said . . .'

'I said, *no* vacancy,' he growled.

Later I found out it was a 'house of ill repute'. That wasn't the career I had in mind.

I found a girls' rooming house at 606 Fourth Street, North. The price was right, so I moved in and promptly made friends with the other girls. Life at 606 was so different from anything I'd ever known. Most of all, it was exciting, being on my own. My room-mate's name was Pinky. She was funny and fun, but also responsible for my oversleeping for one of my three or four jobs. Pinky had left a note saying, 'When you hear the alarm clock out in the hall, it will be time to get up.' Out in the hall? I never figured that one out.

My schedule went something like this: around five a.m. I would return home from Regan's Bakery, where I worked from four p.m. to four a.m. for thirty-five cents an hour. Slicing and wrapping bread became a game to me. I'd do it all in rhythm and run for the cold shower to wake me up when I got tired. Once I got caught in the conveyer belt; it ripped my uniform right off and tried to wrap it. I would sleep until nine a.m., then into the shower, dress and rush to WDAY to rehearse and perform on the Noonday Variety Show for one dollar and fifty cents a show. When I was lucky, Ken would arrange for me to earn another fifty cents a line reading commercials for the big controversy over open-toed versus closed-toed shoes.

There was a short stint in a Greek restaurant as a waitress . . . I always seemed to 'flunk' waitress . . . and I wrote commercials for a local jeweller about love and blue-white diamonds. I also played the role of 'Freckled Face Gertie' on the Hayloft Jamboree with Mary Lou, Jeanne Alm, Ken Kennedy and Howard Nelson, and occasionally sang with Lem Hawkins and the Georgie Porgie Breakfast Food Boys. Lem wanted me to sing 'Sweet Violets', but I drew the line there . . . Doing some filing at WDAY in my spare time was where I found all the good composers and lyricists – Jerome Kern, Otto Harbach, Cole Porter, Rodgers and Hart, Gershwin . . .

One day I received a letter from a childhood friend, Gladys Rasmussen, telling me how beautiful California was. Later, making conversation with my landladies, I threw in, 'I might go to California.' It sounded important, and I very seldom had anything important to say. They said, 'Really? When?'

'Oh, I don't know, I have to . . .' and suddenly the idea

frightened me, I didn't *really* know whether or not I was going to California. I said I had to get my father's permission, although I had long ago stopped asking his permission for anything.

I felt sure he would say no, because California was like going to the moon, or at least to Australia. He surprised me, and gave me not only his permission and blessing, but also a railroad pass. My landladies and all the girls at the rooming house gave me a farewell party, so then I *had* to leave. I sent a telegram to Gladys telling her when I would arrive, and boarded the train.

No sooner had the conductor called out 'All aboard!' than a man, a typical lecher, sat down next to me and began to give me little touches and pats. I was a babe in the woods, only seventeen, and this was my first trip alone, so I didn't know how to handle the situation.

Luckily a woman noticed the hanky-panky going on, came over and said, 'I'll sit by you.' She was fairly large and was wearing an electric-blue dress – she lit up the whole car.

I ended up in the middle, like a sandwich, squeezed in between the man and the woman. She kept poking me with her elbow, the kind of pokes people give you when they want you to notice something, but they always poke a little harder than they need to. After a while I wasn't sure which I disliked more – the pats or the pokes.

This went on until we got to Salt Lake City, where there was a six-hour layover. The lady turned out to be my lifesaver. She took me to the home of some Mormons, who let me have a nice soak in the bathtub, gave me a lovely meal and took me sightseeing. I saw the Mormon Tabernacle and heard the pipe organ; I was enthralled. When I left, they said, 'Now, dear, if you have any trouble getting work or anything in California, you just come back here to us, and we'll take care of you.' I've never forgotten them.

Back on the train the man kept showing me gold nuggets – fool's gold, no doubt . . .

I finally arrived in California, and there on the platform was Gladys Rasmussen and a small welcoming party. The first thing they showed me was Hollywood Boulevard, which at that time was beautifully clean, as polished as someone's marble living room. (I have a star there somewhere now.) Then they took me to have a cheeseburger. I had never even heard of one! All of this was leading up to seeing the Pacific Ocean for the first time. I remember hearing the 'Milkman's Matinée' on the radio in the car . . . I've never had a better cheeseburger, the ocean has never looked so big, and the Hollywood streets never looked so clean.

In Fargo I had sold my graduation watch to my landladies for thirty dollars; by the time I arrived in California, I had only eighteen dollars left. My friend Gladys Rasmussen had even less. She had been working as cashier in the Circus Café, but it had been flooded recently, so she was out of work and broke. I moved into Gladys' rooming house without the landlord's permission, and we would sneak out of there at seven in the morning so we wouldn't be caught – she was behind on the rent. Obviously we had to do some clever thinking until we could pay. We broke the money down so we could each have twenty-five cents a day for the 'big little rib steak' at the Cunningham Diner, plus twenty cents apiece each day for streetcar fares. That enabled us to get to the employment offices in downtown Los Angeles, where we would sit for hours and watch the stream of people going in and out – most of them with jobs.

I looked much younger than my age and didn't seem to qualify for anything they had on offer. When our funds hit an all time low – we had one jar of Laura Scudders peanut butter and one loaf of bread between us – I suddenly lost my shyness, walked up to the desk and said, 'I can do any job you have here.' The lady said there was one left, but it was in Balboa. Could I get there? I certainly could.

Gladys had to stay in Hollywood to guard our room and clothes, and I hitchhiked to Balboa. It turned out to be a short-term job at Harry's Café as a cook and waitress for the Easter break, when the students used to go to Balboa. When I arrived Harry said, 'Have you had any experience?' I decided to be totally honest: 'No, but I learn fast.' (He told me later he decided to give me the job because I was honest.) He found a place for me to stay – a Mr Anderson had rows of little yellow cabins, like enlarged cabanas, so that became home.

Much too soon the Easter break was over, and since I had been making something like nine dollars a week, there wasn't much left. Luckily Mr Anderson also owned the FunZone, and he helped me get work as a barker. My salary was one dollar a day if it didn't rain; it rained a lot!

I discovered a lot of other teenagers in the same impoverished position, but they didn't know as much about survival as I did. I began making a little run every day to get fish – mostly barracuda – from the fishing boats, day-old bread from a bakery, oranges that a nice man let me pick from his trees, and day-old milk from a dairy. You make friends in adversity; we dreamed of pooling our resources and buying an old shell of a boat. We would go out and find abalone, and make those ornaments and pins that said 'Mother Dear'. We didn't get the boat, let alone the abalone, and I'm glad for that, because I never did like those pins that said 'Mother Dear'. Who's supposed to wear them?

I was a shy barker, but people seemed to get a kick out of that, so I developed a regular clientele. The balloon stand had me saying, 'Three for a dime; you break one, you win.' The 'Hit the Wino with the Baseball!' was almost my downfall because I felt so sorry for that man. In carnival language he was known as a 'geek', a man who has gone way beyond caring any more and probably doesn't know where he is. People would throw the baseball which would trigger the mechanism to dump him in the water, and time after time the poor old soul would crawl out and get back on his perch. I never knew his name.

There was also an old lion tamer there who must have done very well because he owned the Ferris wheel and merry-go-round. Everyone had long since stopped caring about his scars, but I was new and was fascinated by them. Every time I let him show me his scars and tell me how he got them he would let me ride on the merry-go-round or Ferris wheel for free. The scars were his identity and he appreciated somebody's caring.

Sometimes when I was off work, I would pose as a customer for the 'Hit the Ducks on the Treadmill' stand. I was pretty good with a slingshot so I could gather a crowd. They didn't pay me any money, but they did give me a big plaster cat, which I was proud of, though I wasn't sure what to do with it. It was my first trophy.

Two guitarists, nephews of one of the concessionaires, used to come to my stand and talk to me about how I got the job, where I was from, where I had worked. They couldn't figure out what I was doing there, because I didn't look or sound like a barker. When I told them I had been a singer at the radio station, they said they would take their guitars out on the pier so I could sing. I was thrilled. I hadn't sung for quite a while.

I'm quite sure they thought I would sing some cowboy song like 'Bury Me Not on the Lone Prairie', but when they asked me what

I wanted to sing, I said, ' "The Man I Love" in A flat.' They were absolutely bowled over that I knew the key. I started to sing and they said, 'Well, you shouldn't be here.' They talked me into hitchhiking back to Hollywood and auditioning at the Jade.

On the way to the Jade my shoe started to come loose on Hollywood Boulevard. I was wearing a beige pant suit made of hopsacking that had had a large colourful silk sash. The tops of my beach shoes had worn and pulled away from the cork soles, and there was no money for new ones. I had cut a piece from the sash and sewed it to the cork sole. It lasted until I started walking towards Highland Avenue, then one shoe started flapping. The other looked as though it would go any minute, and I'd be barefoot. Fortunately, I had a large safety pin in my bag. I raised one foot up on the mailbox and just succeeded in pinning the top to the bottom. It lasted for a couple of blocks, but by then I was at the Jade.

Barefoot, I went in and auditioned for Chuck Barclay, the master of ceremonies, who was tall and terribly handsome. He hired me, thank God. I had literally spent my last dime on a Coca-Cola.

In 1937 the Great Depression was still on. Outside and up the boulevard you could buy a hot dog a mile long for ten cents. Actually, it was a foot long, but even so, that was a lot of hot dog for ten cents, and with the sauerkraut you could call it a meal, as I did.

The Jade had an air of mystery about it, especially to a seventeen-year-old: inside it was dark, with Oriental decor, the smell of the gardenias and Chinese food; the waitresses in their satin coats and pants moved silently on the thick carpet, carrying cooling drinks, egg rolls and butterfly shrimp. An enormous carved dragon formed the bar, where you might see a movie star, an FBI agent, or someone who was looking for a tourist he could 'roll'. I was to learn that expression meant to relieve someone of their bankroll, or at least that was what I thought it meant. You don't forget seeing a confused, stumbling man weaving out the door into the night wondering where his money has gone.

The Jade also had a good reputation for hiring out-of-work entertainers for very little money. Hal March, of *$64,000 Question* fame, was there for a short while. Louis DeProng, long-time choreographer and dance director at 20th Century-Fox; the Brown Sisters, who appeared in the original 'Marie' (before Jack Leonard made it so famous with Tommy Dorsey); Lillian Randolph from The Great Gildersleeve show; Phil Moore, who later became well known as a vocal coach and a bass player (he had kind, brown eyes and said 'swell' a lot), and, of course, Peggy Lee, star of stage, screen and radio . . .

And then there was Jabuti, who had magnificent long red hair, which she used to great advantage as she bumped and ground her near-perfect body over a slide trombone while she played 'Wang Wang Blues', thereby covering an enormous nose and somewhat prominent teeth. Between shows she read big thick books – an intellectual, it seemed.

Louis DeProng used to take pity on me and dance an extra set so I could sit one out when the hour got very late and eat some Chinese food before the long walk home.

Larry Potter, the owner of the Jade, smiled more than most people who have the troubles of a club owner. In his forties, I guessed, he adored his pretty blonde wife, Sue, and the affection certainly seemed mutual. He thought it was charming the way I clenched my fists and left my thumbs stuck up in the air when I sang. Obviously, though, something had to be done about my wardrobe, so Larry took me to the May Company basement to buy a gown, a nice simple one.

One of the most unselfish people there was Mary Norman, a regular singer at the Jade. She gave me a magnificent red-pleated gown to wear, taught me how to apply make-up, and even helped me select my songs. I've always felt bad that suddenly I seemed to have taken her place, without even trying. Mary probably went on to something better – I certainly hope so.

Irene, one of the waitresses, was my guardian. She watched me very closely if she saw me sitting with someone and if they offered me a drink, I was given orange juice.

One evening Larry Potter was sitting with a gentleman I had never seen before – at least, he wasn't a regular customer. He requested that I sit with them and later offered to drive me home. I still can't believe that I was lulled into thinking it would be all right. I was so naïve, to me it seemed only a kind gesture, and the fact that he was sitting with Mr Potter seemed a sort of guarantee. But once I was tucked securely in the car, he started driving in the wrong direction. Even I knew that.

'This is not the right direction,' I said timidly.

'Oh, I just wanted to get something to eat,' he said.

'I'm not a bit hungry. Would you mind just dropping me at home first?'

'Come along, I don't want to eat alone.'

Instinct told me that something was wrong. It had to be an instinct, I didn't seem to have much intelligence going for me. He was going wherever he planned to go, and it was useless to argue. I started to pray.

Somewhere in downtown Los Angeles he stopped in front of a shabby-looking club. He knocked and actually looked through a peephole. Inside there were several people sitting in a booth, who all knew the man who had brought me. (I can't remember his name; let's call him Sam Banks.)

Everyone was drinking, especially Sam. I found myself in the back of the booth sandwiched between two men. The women were gathered around Sam. The man on my left tried to make a little conversation, but I was too frightened to talk and too busy praying. He seemed to understand. We both watched Sam getting drunker by the minute, which this man seemed to think was a little unusual. Suddenly, he whispered to me, 'I'm going to get you out of here. Follow me, stick close.'

We scooted out of the booth, and Sam suddenly loomed up in front of my friend. There was a terrible fight, and fortunately for me, my friend won. The next minute we were rushing out of the club and running for his car.

When we were safely out of the area and he was breathing a little more easily, he said, 'Look, you don't know what you just got away from, but I'm going to tell you. I don't know why I should do this, but you remind me of my little sister. You were headed for white slavery, and nobody would have heard from you again. Nobody.'

I started to cry. He patted my shoulder and said he was going to take me home. I mumbled the address of our rooming house on Gower. 'Promise me you'll never get yourself in a mess like this again. OK? I mean, you're really lucky. You kids running around here trying to be a star . . . Promise me?'

'I promise. I don't want to be a star,' I sobbed.

Chuck Barclay was shocked to hear of my experience, and he and Bob the bartender, Paul the barboy, Irene, Larry and Sue all redoubled their security.

After a while a man began to come in night after night watching me. I liked him, and he seemed to like me, but I was too frightened from the other experience. Then one night he asked if he could drive me home. No. I wouldn't take that chance again.

'Why not?' he said. 'I'm perfectly harmless.'

'Well, I don't really know you.'

'If I get Chuck Barclay to chaperone us, will you let me drive you home?'

'I guess that would be all right,' I said.

In fact we became really good friends. When I saw him again, during World War Two, he was wearing a sailor suit and was about to go to sea. Then in the late forties I was sitting in the assembly at Westlake School for Girls and a friendly voice next to me saying, 'Peggy, I *wondered* when I'd see you again. My daughter is in your daughter Nicki's class.' I asked him why he had seemed so mysterious those many years ago. 'I was a G-man,' he said.

The two dollars a night I earned at the Jade didn't add up to luxurious living. I walked back and forth from our rooming house on Gower to Highland each night, which was about a three-mile stretch. There was a community kitchen in the rooming house, and sometimes one of the other 'hungry' tenants would share a little of our food. So with poor nutrition and the 'after-hours', my health was in a fragile condition. I used to go to the clinic on the corner of Gower and Hollywood Boulevard, and they kept telling me how bad my throat was. One night I fainted. I was taken to the Hollywood Presbyterian Hospital in a squad car. The doctor thought I should go home: 'You don't belong here. You should have surgery, and you need to be near your family.'

It was probably a good idea to go home but I had not told my family where I was because I wanted to wait until I was more successful. I did not write to them until one day when I was caught in a rip-tide and almost drowned.

On the beach Gladys Rasmussen and I would run out with the waves and run back in again. This time I was wearing one of those big housecoats. Gladys was ahead of me and had already run back when the rip-tide – one of those really dangerous waves – filled my housecoat with sand and swept me way out. I never would have believed it would take me out so far.

I was a very good swimmer, but I found I couldn't move, and it was a good thing I didn't try. I never would have made it. Finally, another wave came along, carried me all the way in and threw me on the beach, skinned from head to toe.

This near-drowning made me realize I could have gone and no one would have ever known what happened. That or the white slavery experience would have made me a statistic, just another 'missing person', so I contacted my sisters and they sent Sweeney, my first boyfriend at home, to come and get me. Poor Sweeney was such a handsome, wonderful, caring human being, yet I hardly spoke to him all the way back to North Dakota, to Hillsboro . . . and surgery.

My sister Marianne had been ill with undulant fever, but had bravely been trying to take care of our little family, which consisted of our sister Della, who was now divorced; Tyke, as we called Della's little son Paul; our brother Clair; Ossie Hovde, the nicest 'stray' I ever met; and a mixed-breed dog named Piggie, after the one who went to market.

I found them living in a tiny house in Hillsboro. I hadn't seen them for a long time, not since Nortonville, except for a couple of very short visits. Somehow I couldn't bear to see them struggling along, even though I wasn't in very good shape myself, but in my daydreams – I specialized in daydreams – I would drive up in a big car loaded with gifts for everyone. 'For me?' they would say, and I'd answer, 'Yes, and there's *lots* more.' In later years those daydreams did come true.

Every meal was an adventure – what was it going to be and how were we going to get it – but we loved each other, and that made up for the meagre diet.

Hillsboro was a small town that looked all grey to me. The things I remember most about it were Dr Cuthbert's office (Dr Cuthbert was to operate on my throat) and the way people who saw each other quite often would dress up in clean overalls to come in and get grocery staples and maybe a beer on a Saturday night. The Scandinavians would greet each other with great good humour and say, 'Oh, are yo-o-o-o in town today to-o-o-o?' with a pronounced accent.

I also remember a forty-year-old lady named Frances, who skipped up and down her backyard saying, 'I'll bet you can't do this when you're forty!' (Well, Frances, I vowed to show you, and when I was forty I was flying and dancing all over the world just for starters. Our whole attitude about age changes as the years go by, doesn't it? I never even think of it unless I'm forced to, which I'm convinced is a secret of longevity. It's just *now* all the time.)

I was pondering the philosophy of Frances while Dr Cuthbert, a tall, thin, aristocratic-looking Englishman, who was like a godfather to us, was filling me with something to coagulate my blood in preparation for the throat surgery.

There followed a series of events that resembled a comedy of errors. The first surgery, performed in the doctor's office (there was no hospital), was not a success, and after bringing me home Dr Cuthbert had to rush back on an emergency basis. He tried holding clamps in my throat, leaning over the bed, while the dog Piggie chewed his leg, trying to protect me. He could not stop the hae-morrhaging, so he propped me up in the back seat of the car, with a large pan in my lap and my sister Della next to me, bug-eyed and pale with fright. He drove as fast as he could go from Hillsboro to the Deaconess Hospital in Grand Forks.

He had called in advance, and they were prepared for surgery. I was given transfusions, and Della kept saying, 'You look like you're made of wax.' I assured her I was not.

While recuperating, I did a lot of thinking about my family and life in general. It was one of those bitter cold times in Grand Forks. Looking out of the window at the chunks of frozen slush sprinkled with fresh snow, I watched a little sparrow hop around chirping cheerfully as he pecked away at some horse manure. I remember thinking, 'If that little sparrow can make it, I can make it too.'

I started to get well and to plan how to move my little family to Fargo.

Back in Fargo I re-established my contacts at WDAY and, with Ken Kennedy's help, talked to the Powers family, the owners of the Powers Hotel and Coffee Shop. There had been no live entertainment in Fargo, perhaps nowhere in North Dakota, but there was a good organist named Lloyd Collins who played up on a little riser in the Coffee Shop. I was soon up there with him.

The Powers Hotel was considered *the* hotel in town, and the Coffee Shop was the favoured spot of the college students. They were hungry for entertainment, and we were soon jammed to the rafters. I answered as many as ninety or a hundred requests during an evening, especially for 'The Music Goes 'Round and 'Round' and 'Deep in a Dream'.

Lloyd Collins boned up on all of the songs of the favourite composers I mentioned earlier, plus Johnny Mercer, who was not only a favourite lyricist ('I Thought About You') but later became my mentor when I began writing songs.

My salary was only fifteen dollars a week for six days plus a Sunday matinée performance of semi-classical songs such as 'Would God I Were a Tender Apple Blossom' and Tom Powers' favourite, 'I'll Take You Home Again, Kathleen'. I took her home again quite a few times . . .

By this time I had found the Hogan Apartments, within walking distance of WDAY and just down the street from the Powers Coffee Shop. Oh, happy day, when I sent for the family from Hillsboro! The apartment was in a burned-out building, so it was a good thing we were all so inventive. With paint and brushes, needle and thread, polish and shine, we made the best of it and celebrated our first Christmas together since the house burned down in Jamestown.

We had guests from all walks of life: doctors, lawyers, day workers, college students, newspaper writers, ice skaters. I used to keep a guest book until it got me in trouble with my boyfriends. We celebrated one birthday for three full days. I recall Bob Donahue, who worked at the Fargo Forum, kept getting back in line for a birthday kiss.

There was my friend Johnny Quam, who was really important in my life – he worked at a dry-cleaning shop and could keep my 'other dress' clean. Seriously, though, I really liked Johnny, and when he bought tickets for *Gone with the Wind*, I thought we had hit the big time. I planned what I was going to wear just as though I had a choice.

With my puny earnings, every once in a while I would fall behind with the rent; I would go downstairs to see Mrs Hogan and play a schottische for her on the piano. She was mad for schottisches and would extend the rent time.

Meanwhile, we were doing so well at the Powers Coffee Shop that Le Chateau, the rival hotel, imported a singer from Minneapolis! Jane Leslie Larrabee turned out to be one of the best friends I've had in my life, and later, by introducing her to Leonard Feather, the noted jazz critic, I did her a good turn: they are still happily married.

When Jane arrived we were supposed to be in competition. I thought she was the cat's pyjamas. I had seen her in Grand Forks at the Belmont Café. She was so pretty and had the biggest soft brown eyes. We met seriously in Fargo. She was, she says, sizing me up, and I was probably doing the same; we weren't supposed to like each other, I guess, but we did.

My fans – bless them – were always making little remarks like, 'Well, she didn't have near the people you had,' or, 'She's OK, but I like your singing better.' Secretly, I enjoyed that a little, but that's only human. Jane and I happily sent each other customers, thereby greatly increasing the night life in Fargo – Le Chateau flourished as well as the Powers Coffee Shop.

I *loved* Janie's clothes. Of course, I had so little – 'that one' and 'the other one'. She knew I was working almost around the clock and that my wardrobe didn't extend all the way around, so that nice girl just said straight out, 'Would you like to borrow some of my clothes?' I had never heard of such a thing, and I can still feel the rush of gratitude I felt then.

It was so good to have a friend I could share my troubles with. Trying to support my family wasn't easy. Marianne kept house and cooked the meals while Della, who was bedridden for eight years, read book after book. Clair couldn't seem to find employment. Once in a while he and his friend Murphy found a bit of Sunnybrook, however, and come home with fumes of whiskey trailing behind them.

Fifteen dollars a week was not enough to feed six people – Della, Tyke, Clair, Marianne, Ossie Hovde and myself – but I was grateful for the work, and I enjoyed singing. I did some funny things to earn little luxuries. One night on a bet I chewed five packs of Beaman's Pepsin chewing gum (until then my favourite flavour) to win a carton of 'tailor-made' cigarettes for Della and Clair. My jaws ached for days and days. And I loved it when we all went on a picnic. To fill the basket full of potato salad, homemade, of course, dill pickles, bologna sandwiches, fried chicken, cookies or cake, watermelon and lemonade, and go down by the river and spread out the picnic. Cucumbers and onions – oh, yes, the smells of summer . . .

Eventually Janie went back to Minneapolis. I really missed her, but we kept writing letters, and one day Ken Kennedy said, 'I think I can get you a job with my cousin, Sev Olson, in Minneapolis. Would you like that?' *Would I like that?* Except for one thing – the idea of leaving my family behind. It had to be done sometime, I knew, but I cried for weeks. They were pretty upset, too, except dear Marianne, who always understood everything. She got a job working for a doctor, and I left for Minneapolis.

I auditioned for Sev Olson, singing 'Body and Soul', but I'll bet he and Ken had it all set. Before I knew it, I was living in the Radison Hotel, which was heaven to me. I'd plough around in those thick carpets and lose my appetite, overcome by the grandeur.

Sev Olson was my first big crush. He was handsome and kind and funny; I was practically dizzy just being around him, and he unfortunately shared my feelings. He would break into hives. I knew I was in deep water now and kept wondering what I would do to get away. There was no hope for it right from the start, because he was married.

The fellows in the band were all so nice – Willy Peterson, Max, Nooky Norgaard – and all of them guessed what was happening, I'm sure, but they were as discreet as possible. They were university students, as was Sev, but he was my knight in shining armour!

I talked to Jane and to Jane's mother, Tody, about it. They were both fond of Sev and didn't quite know how to advise me. I spent the next few months between pleasure and pain, until Will Osborne came to town with his orchestra. Then I made my decision. I auditioned for Will, singing 'I Can't Give You Anything But Love', and he said that I had the job. It really hurt me to do it, but one night I couldn't stand it any longer so I told Sev.

He brought his wife Martie down to where we were playing, and we all wound up crying as they told me she was willing to give him up. But deep inside I knew it was wrong to continue with the relationship, so I stuck to my guns and tearfully told them I would be leaving in the morning. I didn't dare let any time elapse. He could so easily have talked me out of it. I am glad to know that they are still together.

The next day I set out into the larger world with Gene Nelson and his wife in their car. Gene was a trombone player and the back seat was full of musical instruments. There I was in the middle again, with the heater blowing in my face.

As we drove along, I told them the story about the owner of the Marigold Ballroom, who was always coming up to Sev on the bandstand and telling him to play something fast. One time Sev said, 'We just played something fast!' to which the owner replied, 'Well, that's not fast enough. You've got to remember, Sev, this is a big ballroom and by the time it gets to the other end, it's too slow!'

It seemed like forever before we got to St Louis. Our booking at the beautiful, enormous Fox Theatre extended into the new year. On New Year's Eve, just before they called 'half hour', all the lights went out, and a robbery took place in the box office. We were calling to each other from floor to floor, 'Do you have any candles?' We didn't have any electricity for the spot lights, but we all tried to put our make-up on by the light of matches, flashlights and candles, and then walked downstairs in the dark, trying to keep track of what floor we were on. It was very exciting. For some reason none of us thought about any danger – that it might be an armed robbery – we just carried on, and the audience was wonderful, joining in to help us save the day.

One morning I woke up and I felt a lump in my throat. I went to a doctor and had the nerve to ask him if he could excise it. Dr Brown actually tried to do it then and there, but he had to give up and told me to come back for surgery the next day.

I was trying to be so brave that I overdid it. I was alone in the operating room with the anaesthetist, which didn't strike me as odd then, but it does now. I asked, 'Could I have gas instead of ether? Ether makes me so sick.' He didn't answer. I tried it again. He was gathering his implements or whatever and seemed annoyed. This time he walked over to me and quite deliberately pushed me down on the table. I had been sitting there swinging my legs casually to look sophisticated and show him I wasn't afraid. Now there was no more pretence. He fastened the straps, put the ether cone over my nose and mouth and began pouring, not dripping, the ether on to the gauze. I was fighting to stay conscious as I felt the ether dribbling down the side of my face.

'Where are they?' I screamed silently. 'Where is Doctor Brown?' I frantically wiggled my fingers to show them I was awake. I was hearing those weird flapping sounds again, and I continued to fight to stay awake. Finally, I heard them coming in the door . . .

Before I opened my eyes, I kept pulling at my mouth, and Max Schall, the band manager, said soothingly, 'Don't pull those, Peggy, they're stitches. You've had a little accident . . .'

I certainly had! By the time the ether wore off, I was asking for a mirror and not getting one. Finally, I remembered my purse was in the drawer next to me. The mirror revealed a horrible sight: my nose was swollen, the front teeth had been broken off as they went through my lower lip, and somehow I had managed to cut my tongue. With a strange kind of speech caused by the stitches in my tongue and lip, I was calling out, 'Oook what ey id to me!'

A nurse came in, thought I'd been in a car accident, and after patting me, walked out the door.

Finally, Max came back and explained it all. It seems that when they were moving me from the table to the cart, they dropped me on the hard floor – I think it was marble tile – and I landed on my face.

The nuns came to visit me and told me the hospital was built by charity, and I shouldn't punish the hospital for the actions of one man who obviously was not well. I was glad to be alive, so I signed. Anyway I wasn't of age. I'm glad I signed, but the damage has cost a bundle since then.

Dr Brown arranged for a dentist to cap my teeth, and as soon as I was well, Max Schall, Hank the pianist and I took off for California by car, Will Osborne's band having broken up while I was in hospital.

Beautiful California again! We finally made it there after a frightening experience in the mountains just outside of Globe, New Mexico. There was a stretch of new road, which, after pouring rain, was a sheet of mud. We were stuck there with hundreds of other cars for hours until a tow truck managed to pull us out car by car.

I went back to the Jade to be welcomed with open arms by Chuck Barclay, Irene, Bob the bartender and Paul the barboy, and, of course, Sue and Larry Potter. Max helped me find an apartment in Whitley, in Hollywood, which was close to the Jade.

A songwriter named Jack Brooks, who had written 'Once Upon A Dream' and much later 'Ole Buttermilk Sky' and 'That's Amore', took a special interest in my singing. He thought the Doll House in Palm Springs would be a wonderful place for me to sing.

The Doll House was originally the home of some folks named

Doll. They started serving dinners because Palm Springs didn't have many, if any, restaurants then. Mr Wrigley, of the Spearmint gum fortune, loved that sunny place and the story goes that he used to say, 'Let's go to the Doll House for dinner.' The name stuck and it became a very popular spot for world travellers and movie stars. I recognized Franchot Tone, Peter Lorre, James Cagney, Jack Benny, Dennis Day and many others, but only Franchot Tone and Peter Lorre talked with me.

The Guadalajara Trio was very popular there, and now and then I'd sing along with them . . . 'Tonight will live forever.' I can still hear them.

One night Freddie and Lois Mandel came to the Doll House. Freddie owned the Detroit Tigers and Mandel's department store in Chicago. They arranged an audition and brought Frank Bering to hear me. Bering was a partner of Ernie Byfield and they owned the Ambassador East and West in Chicago.

It was closing time when they arrived, and the musicians had gone. 'Well,' I said, 'there's a group down at Claridge's called The Four Of Us. They'll play for me.' We went down there to find they'd already packed their instruments, but they took them out and played while I sang 'The Man I Love'.

At Bering's request I went to Chicago. Bering said, 'I'm hiring you more because of your enthusiasm than anything else.' I wonder why that impressed me. It wasn't exactly a compliment.

The logistics of getting from point A to point B were interesting. I believe Freddie and Lois gave me a ticket to get to Chicago from Palm Springs. Some kind soul gave me a ride to Los Angeles, and the point of departure was Union Station. In the meantime, I had called Jane Leslie Larrabee, told her of my good fortune and asked her to meet me in Chicago. She agreed.

When I arrived at the Ambassador West (I was to sing in the Buttery there), I found the lobby was even more luxurious than the Radison, and self-consciousness flooded my face.

'Will you please write your residence on the register?' the clerk asked.

'Oh, yes, of course,' I stuttered and then became confused because I really didn't have a home at that point. 'Well, I guess it's here.' I shrugged, trying to be nonchalant. (I wished he'd drop the subject.)

In the end the clerk convinced me it could be my last home

address, and I was taken to a lovely suite. It was so nice that I stayed dressed up all the time. Janie arrived, and she did the same.

The Mandels had arranged for the beautiful rooms at the Ambassador, and for me to get half off on anything I bought in the hotel. Mlle Oppenheimer would furnish my gowns and wardrobe. Every day a maid would come with a beautiful gown on a hanger and anything else I wanted to wear. It seemed like a fairy tale come true.

I also got seventy-five dollars a week for spending money, plus all my room service paid. But at first we were unaware of the room-service arrangement and as a result nearly starved to death. Janie's mother, Tody, had sent some delicious date-filled cookies, which we ate right down to the last crumb. Other than that, we had a *very* small amount of money left between us for White Tower hamburgers. Two of the hotel chambermaids, Iris and Tillie, came to the rescue. They began bringing us coffee and rolls and whatever else they found on the room service tables.

About fifteen or twenty years later I came back to sing at the Chicago Civic Opera House with a musical review and had a suite at the Ambassador West. Iris and Tillie were still there, so we had coffee together and I was able to ask them, 'How did you know we were starving? We didn't *tell* you.' Tillie, in her sunny Irish way, said, 'Well, we didn't see nothin' going in, and we didn't see nothin' going out!'

Back in 1941 I was treated like Eloise in the hotel, and the Mandels gave a party at their home to introduce me to Chicago society. I tasted my first champagne, and I didn't say, 'It tickles my nose.' I just got sick. But what a wonderful whirl, with all those lovely gowns; it still sparkles in my memory.

Late at night after I sang I would go to Rush Street and hear Laura Ricker and Baby Dodds – two of the old-time greats. Laura played the piano and sang, Baby sang and played the drums. Laura eventually went completely blind. She was losing her sight then, but she taught me to sing songs like 'Let's Do It'. Baby Dodds sang songs he had composed. His brother, Johnny Dodds, was a famous jazz musician of the old school, and Baby had written a blues for him when he died: 'Blues for you, Johnny, I hang my head and cry . . .' I don't remember any more of it, but it was a very moving song. They both had quite an effect on me; I loved them very much.

3

Big Band

I didn't intend to be a jazz singer, and even now I don't know what kind of singer I am, but Louis Armstrong said I always knew how to swing. He wrote it on a photograph he gave me. I'm proud of that. It's true I always understood about swinging – I remember clapping our hands the first day in school, and I could do it. There were only a couple of us in the class who could – I wonder why.

It was in Chicago that I got my first big break with Benny Goodman. Word was getting around about the new singer at the Buttery, thanks to people like Morty Palitz, one of the executives from Columbia Records, and famous bandleaders like Claude Thornhill, Glenn Miller and Charlie Barnett, who came there.

Jazz pianist Mel Powell was playing with Benny Goodman's band at the College Inn in Chicago, and he accompanied Benny and Lady Duckworth, who later became Alice Goodman, the night they came to hear me sing. At the time Benny was the most popular musician in the world, and Helen Forrest, his girl singer, was about to leave his band.

They all settled down at a table and ordered steak. Mel Powell would later tell me that when I came on stage and started singing 'These Foolish Things', Benny mumbled, 'I guess we've got to get somebody for Helen.' Mel thinks he decided to hire me on the spot.

It certainly didn't look that way to me. The musicians I was working with, 'The Four of Us', were excited that he was in the audience, but I was sure he didn't like me: he just stared at me and chewed his tongue. (I later learned that was just preoccupation.)

Helen Forrest, who was probably the most popular vocalist of the day, was moving to Artie Shaw's band. Maybe it was over money, but the world of popular music was a small one in those days, and it wasn't unusual for big band vocalists to move around from band to band, sometimes returning to the same one in a few months' time. Some of the top big band soloists in the 1940s included Doris Day, Frank Sinatra and Dick Haymes. Dick replaced Frank in Harry James' band when Frank went on to Tommy Dorsey, just

Momma and Daddy.

Della, Marianne, Norma (Peggy), and Jeannie.

My beloved sister, Marianne.

Daddy's last picture just before he died.

Ken Kennedy, programme director at WDAY.
He's the one who named me Peggy Lee.

Sev Olsen and his orchestra from Minneapolis.
Sev was my first serious romance.

Miss Peggy Lee and the big brass at WDAY.

'Miss Peggy Lee' as I was officially known...
(Photo credit: Richard Olson)

Peggy and Nicki.

*With Mel Torme, having fun
on a television show.*

Johnny Mercer, Peggy Lee, and Glen Wallichs. I'd just won the
1946 Down Beat Award. (Photo credit: Gene Lester)

Composing music with Dave Barbour. (Photo credit: Gene Howard)

Peggy, Nicki and Dave Barbour. (Photo credit: Charlie Mihn)

The Paramount Theatre in New York City
where Dave and I were performing.

Peggy and Woody Herman doing a radio show.

Peggy, Jimmy Durante and Arthur Treacher in the Santa Claus Parade, 1947. (Photo credit: Hollywood Pictorial Service)

The recording session for 'Mañana' with Dave Barbour and Carmen Miranda's rhythm section. They marched out of the studio playing 'Mañana'. (Photo credit: Gene Howard)

Louis Armstrong, Frank Sinatra, Peggy Lee and Bing Crosby.

A head shot from the 1950s.

Peggy Lee and Nat King Cole.

as Helen was now going from Benny to Artie Shaw. Helen's leaving
meant that Benny's floor show at the College Inn was going to be
without its star band vocalist. Lesser bands, like Claude Thornhill's,
always needed an established star-singer to help draw crowds, but
Benny Goodman was so successful on his own that he could go for
what he wanted, and never mind 'name-power'.

The next day Jane told me Benny Goodman called. I refused to
believe her.

'You have to believe me!' Jane said. 'It was Benny Goodman's
voice. He wants you to call him about working for him.'

'Oh, I can't believe that. He was in the Buttery, and I saw the
look on his face. He couldn't have liked me – '

'Well, I'm telling you he called, and you should return the call.
Don't be silly! What can you lose – even if it's a joke?'

'You're right. I'll call him, but what do I say?'

'Just tell him you're returning his call. I'm sure it was Benny
Goodman.'

'OK, you're right. What can I lose?'

I dialled the number. 'Hello. This is Peggy Lee. Is Mr Goodman
there?'

'This is Mr Goodman.'

'Oh – did you call me?'

'Yes, I did. I want to know if you'd like to join my band?'

Well, he didn't even ask me to have a rehearsal with him; he just
said, 'Come to work and wear something pretty.' When I put the
phone down, I still couldn't believe it was true. 'Somebody's just
playing a joke,' I insisted to Jane. After all, Benny Goodman was
one of my fantasy figures – I spent money I didn't have on 'Don't
Be That Way' in the jukebox when I was working in Balboa.

I arrived at work in a nice dress, as requested, and there was no
rehearsal. Mel Powell was there and, God bless him, he was such a
help to me. Someone told me what songs I would be singing, and
luckily I knew them all. Mel would give me four bars and I would
count and listen hard for where I was supposed to come in – jumping
in at the last moment, hoping for the best.

Mel's version of the story goes like this:

'Peggy must have been a nervous wreck. Her first assignment was
to make a recording. Columbia Records, to whom Benny was contrac-
ted, always came out to wherever the band was playing. So they
arrived in Chicago to record. There Peg was, making a recording

with Benny Goodman just a day or two after she joined the band.

'She met CBS producer John Hammond in the control room, and he handed her the sheet music for "Elmer's Tune". This was a pretty tough rap for a kid. There was no taping in those days. You just made records. If you blew something, you started from the beginning. You didn't say, "Well, let's take it from measure 39 and splice it." She was so nervous. The sheet music John handed her made such a racket, and they didn't have high-tech ways of beating that, so, unfortunately, it sounded like a forest fire that was going over the brass, over the saxophones.

'Peggy had probably been up all night learning this thing, and then she came in, and the arrangement was disorienting because "Elmer's Tune" was very clever, very fancy, full of stuff.

'I led her into an adjacent studio and we sat down and ran through a couple of things that were in the arrangement, especially the cues for her, and it was sort of like bop-bop-ba-tump-de-tump. I was constantly cueing her about where she came in, and told her that during the recording of the arrangement I could always improvise something.

'I also told her, "You're going to have your first tone, Benny won't know, nobody will know. I'm just gonna pop that in there in the midst of what seems to be just a ramble over the band while the band's playing. You catch it from that; that'll be cue, count four, and go." Well, I think she's never forgotten it.'

I started singing with the Goodman band in the middle of their College Inn engagement in Chicago. With no rehearsal, I was so nervous I thought the spotlight was alive. I would sit there until Mel cued me, then I would start counting and come in wherever Eddie Sauter's modulation had taken us. I don't think it ever occurred to Benny that singers, who have to memorize everything, need a rehearsal (he did have us rehearse on regular rehearsal days, but this was something quite different) – you can't walk up to the microphone with a sheet of music in your hand. The musicians have theirs, but the singer has nothing but what she or he is hearing or has memorized.

That first night with Benny I remember singing 'My Old Flame'. The critics were cruel. They captioned a photo of me in *Downbeat* magazine, 'Sweet Sixteen and will never be missed'. I had a cold, and I was singing in Helen Forrest's key. I went to Benny and said, 'I'd like to quit, please.'

He just looked at me. 'I won't let you.'

So I stayed with Benny, though it did mean taking a decrease in salary, and there were no more lavish gowns from Mlle Oppenheimer. But there were great career advantages. Advantages for Benny as well, because I had in my possession a wind-up phonograph and a recording by Lil Green called 'Why Don't You Do Right?' Benny paid me ten dollars for recording 'Why Don't You Do Right?' and no royalties. My weekly salary was seventy-five dollars, out of which I had to pay for my own room and board. 'Why Don't You Do Right?' became the biggest-selling record in America when we released it a couple of years later. It stayed there for a long time and still sells.

After the College Inn, we did some one-nighters. On the road with Benny, Mel and I would ride together in the bus and sing – he'd sing the brass parts sometimes, and I'd sing the reeds, or vice versa, to things like 'Down South Camp Meeting', 'Stealin' Apples'. I knew the parts from listening on the stand every night.

We'd sing and pass the miles away. We went to Toronto for some kind of exposition. They would just tell me when the bus was leaving, and I would pack my laundry, damp or dry, and hope I wouldn't catch a cold because of my wet hair – we didn't have portable driers then; at least, I didn't.

After that we were on our way to New York. The Big Apple!

When I arrived in New York in 1941 the bellman brought my luggage and led me to the door of my first Manhattan residence, in the Victoria Hotel. Morty Palitz had said, 'Now, don't stay at the Forrest. All the musicians stay there, and I want you to keep out of trouble. The Victoria is a nice, respectable place for a young woman, and the rent isn't too bad.'

I hurried to the window and looked out. Way down below were cabs and cars moving along. The Black Building in Fargo, ND, was eight storeys high, and until now that was as high as I'd ever been, except once when Ole Olson had flown me in a Curtis Robin bi-wing plane all over the green patches of Dakota farmland. I had wanted to be up high so badly I had even danced the Charleston for him – right there in the field. And, just as I had looked in awe over the side of that little plane, I now looked out the window of the Victoria and gasped at all I could see . . . The Roseland Ballroom sign was blinking at me – ROSELAND, ROSELAND, ROSELAND. I felt a little tickle in the pit of my stomach and backed away from the window for a minute. But then I was back again, looking, looking . . .

The band was going to play the New Yorker Hotel. In 1941 the New Yorker was a really luxurious hotel, or so it seemed to me. It certainly was a busy place, people whipping and whirling around through the revolving doors.

Then the magic of walking into the Terrace Room when the sparkling Ice Show was finished, sitting on the same stage with Benny Goodman, and hearing the band play 'Don't Be That Way' – not the jukebox. Here I was on the bandstand with those brilliant musicians behind me – Mel Powell, Jimmy Maxwell, Big Sid Catlett, Cootie Williams, Billy Butterfield, Cutty Cutshall, Miff Mole, Hymie Schertzer – watching all those people dance by. Some were stars I could recognize, and I pulled my feet under my gown and stared my heart out.

Every night the room was charged with electricity for me, although some would have said the cold Scandinavian never felt any of that. Later they called me 'cool', which suited me just fine. I was to learn there was a rule about the musicians not fraternizing with the girl singer, but we all became friends in spite of it.

Soon Benny was taking me to 52nd Street to catch some of the other acts in town, and one night we went to hear Fats Waller and sat through set after set. When Fats came over to our table, it was the first time I ever asked anyone for his autograph. Fats took out an ace of spades and signed it for me.

There was also a writer named George Simon who was around a lot when I sang with Benny. He was one of the 'Simon & Schuster' Simons – Carly Simon's uncle. We started dating, but then I met Peter Dean, whom I absolutely adored. A singer and an ad man – and what a charmer. They even called him 'Snake Hips' because of a dance he did when he sang.

One night at the New Yorker, I was singing 'That Did It, Marie' when Count Basie danced by the stage. He winked up at me and said, 'Are you sure you don't have a little spade in you, Peggy?' I also met Louis and Lucille Armstrong at this time, and it was love at first sight. Duke Ellington came to hear me, and later nicknamed me 'The Queen'. And that stuck until years later, when the disc jockey William B. Williams christened me 'The Elegant One'.

Thanks, fellows.

★　　★　　★

One evening a handsome RAF pilot limped into the Terrace Room and was seated at a table right next to the bandstand. I couldn't help but look at him and wondered why he was limping. When we finished our set, I walked by his table and asked if he'd like some company. We were encouraged to do that in those days. He asked me to sit down, told me he was a fan of Benny's and that he was enjoying my singing.

I noticed he kept requesting sad songs, one of which was Cole Porter's 'Begin the Beguine' – that seemed to be his favourite. I was uneasy – although not quite sure why; but he had such a tentative air about him. If I tried a joke, he would only smile as though to thank me for trying. Finally he told me about joining the RAF. He was from Illinois, but had volunteered to help England (we weren't yet in the war).

We spent the whole evening together, between sets, and when we were finished and were about to say goodnight, I felt myself trying to arrange another time with him . . . like the next day, Saturday lunch when we did our matinée after the Ice Show. He agreed.

I was just a minute or two late for our date and he called my room. 'Where are you? Aren't you coming down?' 'Yes,' I said, 'I'll be right there. I'm sorry.'

He had bought me a bracelet from the gift shop in the hotel. I was so surprised and felt reluctant to accept it, until he said, 'Please, you've been so good to me. It's just a thank you.' I took it, but wondered what he meant that I'd been so good to him.

After lunch I returned to the bandstand and we played 'Begin the Beguine' again for him. When the luncheon set was over, he came upstairs with me and began to tell me of his deepest feelings – how he thought he would never get over having killed people. He said he couldn't go back in to the service again because of the injury, but he didn't really want to because he was plagued with the memory of the bombs he had dropped on people – innocent people. Was he a coward?

'No,' I said. 'Of course you're not. You've just been through something pretty terrible . . .'

'But what do I do with my life now? I'm a coward and a . . .' He gestured to his injured leg.

'Maybe you could be a commercial pilot,' I said weakly, and he gave me a wistful smile as if to say, 'You just don't understand.' I didn't.

After we had made a date to have dinner together and meet in the Terrace Room, he suddenly said, 'I want to give you these,' and he took off his wings.

I was taken aback and said, 'You're not supposed to take these off unless . . .' and fell silent. He gave them to me with that odd, sad smile, and I said, 'I'll keep them for you.'

This time I rushed so I wouldn't be late for dinner, but he was already there. He seemed distant. We didn't order dinner; we just talked idly about Benny and the band, and suddenly I realized it was time to go back to work. I excused myself to go to the powder room and smiled at him. 'Be right back,' I said as I left.

I came out of the powder room a few minutes later and realized there was something in the air. One of the girls who worked at the hotel said, 'Isn't it terrible about that young pilot?'

Well, I *knew*. I ran out of the Terrace Room. The phone was ringing in my room. It was Benny, and he said, 'Don't talk to anyone. That pilot you've been talking to just shot himself through the head.'

Shock. Benny saying, 'Come down and go to work. It will do you good.'

'Oh, Benny, I can't.'

'Come down right now.'

Alec Wilder and Freddy Goodman fed me cognac, and I managed to sing in some strange manner.

The next day the pilot's brother came to New York to make arrangements. He told me he had been talking to him on the phone when he shot himself. Although he was in shock too, he made me feel a lot better. 'You mustn't blame yourself for anything,' he said. 'I'm just glad you made his last hours as pleasant as you could.'

I gave the wings and his identification tag to his brother to give to his mother and dad. There was nothing else to do but say a prayer for him.

After the first New Yorker engagement, we went out for more one-nighters. Mel Powell and I added 'Clarinet à la King' to the songs we sang on the bus. Meanwhile Mel was writing such pieces as 'Mission to Moscow' and 'The Earl' – what a mind! We had a lot of fun together. He tells this story about me from that time.

'The band was very successful, and we would charter trains to travel around. My room-mate at the time was a fellow named George Berg. We'd become good friends and would share a compartment on a train. A lot of guys in the band were, if not utterly crazed, at least moderately looney. But we were peace-loving guys and attempted to stay somewhat by ourselves.

'We were in Pittsburgh – next stop St Louis – and had finished the date early. It was about eleven o'clock, and we had the luxury of a little time, because we weren't due to leave until 2.00 a.m.

'George, who'd been on the road a thousand years, proposed that we go to a special ribs place, pick up a couple of portions, go down to the train yard and get aboard our cars early. Nobody would be there; we'd just sit quietly. It would be a pleasure.

'Now, George used to be a big fan of marijuana. He never drank, just marijuana, very pure, whereas for me a couple of shots of Scotch would do the trick nicely. So I thought, "Terrific. After a hard night's work, we'll go out there and get rested, nobody to bother us. If the other guys wanted to get loaded, let them."

'We got out to the railroad yard only to discover it absolutely deserted. After stumbling around in the dark we somehow located one of the two coaches with "Benny Goodman" painted on the side.

'We found the little drawing-room we were to share, got undressed and into pyjamas, and took out the ribs. George began to smoke his marijuana; I had a couple of drinks. We were just congratulating ourselves on our farsightedness, revelling in our aloneness, when suddenly there was a knock at the door.

'We jumped a foot. Shaken, I went to the door, opened it, and there was Peg, terror stricken, panicked, in tears. Now I was really unnerved.

' "What's the matter, Peg?"

'She could hardly speak. "I came out early – wanted to be alone and relax . . ."

' "Yes," I said.

' "I went to my room . . . and there's a dead body."

'It was the dead of night, she was hysterical, the band wasn't due for an hour and a half. We'd all seen too many movies; you've got to be a hero . . .

' "Wait, I'll get my slippers," I said.

'She put her hand in mine. She was trembling. We walked down the little corridor to her compartment, and I sort of peeked in, already beginning to get weak-kneed, knowing right then that I was not a dead-body man, and I saw a head – covered with blood. So it was not just a question of a dead body. There'd been bad business here. I looked around, and I didn't see the body.

' "It's in my closet. Mel, I didn't even notice the head." Peg was blubbering.

' "Are you kidding?" I said. It was on the floor. Yet it seems she'd actually missed it, had gone to hang up her coat, opened the door of her closet . . .

' "Look, Babes, I think what we've got to do is jog down to the station, it's about a quarter of a mile, and talk to someone, tell the police or something."

' "Well, gee, I wish you could get it out of here for me," she said.

' "Peg, are you crazy? I don't want to get near a thing like this," I said, beginning to back out the door. Just then a couple of the guys, obviously feeling the other side of marvellous, arrived: Freddy Goodman, Benny's brother, who was road manager for the band, and Lou McGarrity, a trombone player.

' "What's the matter?" Freddy said, and before anyone could say anything, he saw. "What the hell's going on here?"

' "There's a body in the closet!" Peggy yelled.

'They were right behind me, the corridor was small, and suddenly they've shoved me back into the room and we're all right in front of the closet – Freddy on my right, McGarrity on my left, Peggy behind us, sobbing.

' "Wait!" I began, but Freddy was already opening the door. I'm three inches from the cadaver, and I don't want to look, so I turn my head away just as it begins to fall on me. I feel this tremendous body weight, this dead weight, and I'm pushing against it in absolute revulsion, and I hear Peggy yell, "Mel, watch out! It's falling!"

'Horrified, I try to back off, but it's too heavy, and I go down with it on top of me, and, oh God, I'm trapped on the floor, and I'm about to have a coronary, when I hear laughter – from the *cadaver*. At last I look, and it's Sid Weiss, the bass player. He's wild, shaking, and catsup from his face is dripping on mine.

'Peggy had *set it up*. She'd staged the whole damned thing, and now she was screaming, and Sid Weiss was picking me up from the floor, too stunned to think, yet wondering even then at the labyrinth plans the woman had gone to.

'Still, even as I tell the story, the image that most clearly remains with me is this – a pair of slippers aligned perfectly outside Peg's door in the corridor – George Berg's slippers. My friend, in a marijuana haze, had obviously seen what he supposed was a headless thing drop out from Peg's closet and jumped clean out of his slippers.'

I planned this little ghoulish joke because the fellows used to tease me so. Every time an accident happened, somehow I was always there to see it. I would come into work and say, 'Guess what happened to me today.' They would look at each other as if to say, 'Sure, we know.' Sid Weiss was the right size to fit into the closet, so I just talked him into it. They didn't tease me after that.

Benny was always a bit preoccupied, like the absent-minded professor, but there was something lovable about him too. Mel Powell's wife once said, 'The question with Benny is whether the plug is *in* or out.' I remember Benny playing 'The World is Waiting for the Sunrise' in a crowded ballroom one night when a girl who was jammed up against the bandstand listening fainted dead away. Benny kept playing with his eyes shut, and I doubt if he noticed as we got help to carry the girl out in the air.

Benny and I took the plane to our next stop, and it was a *bumpy* prop flight. Everyone on the plane except Benny and I was sick to their stomach. Lots of those bags passed around. When we finally landed, there was a limo waiting, but neither Benny nor I knew where we were going. Fortunately, the driver remembered seeing an advertisement about where we were playing . . .

There are hundreds of such stories, but I'll never forget him going into a burger place and ordering a hot dog. The waitress said, 'We don't have any hot dogs.' He replied, 'But I'm Benny Goodman.' She said, 'We *still* don't have any hot dogs.'

In between these one-nighters, Janie Larrabee and I found an apartment in Greenwich Village on 12th Street. It had not one but *two* fireplaces, and we just flipped. We set about keeping house; I bought a peck of potatoes, which she found very amusing, and I also bought a bag of flour, some yeast and other ingredients for making bread. We had an absolutely wonderful time buying pillows for our couches, towels for our bathroom, which we cleaned and shined.

Meanwhile I was falling a little in love with a Flying Tiger from General Chennault's American Volunteer Group. (With the war looming it was easy to do that because you were afraid to let them go, afraid you'd never see them again!)

When we first met Frank was stationed in Washington, DC. I would manage to get down to see him on my day off, and he would come to New York whenever he could. It seemed as though we were always meeting in a crowded station and always planning our wedding. One time, I had set the bread and put it in the warm closet to rise before I left for Washington. I stayed a little longer than expected, and I got a frantic call from Janie asking me what she should do with the bread dough that was spreading all over the closet! I caught the next train.

Frank and I got engaged. We had the rings, the licence and all. The band was playing a theatre in Bridgeport, Connecticut, and I was to meet Frank in New York the next day. During our half hour, Frank managed to get a call to me to tell me he couldn't meet me as arranged because they were flying out on a secret mission. I was shocked and, I thought, brokenhearted.

I stood there, staring straight ahead, and Joe Rushton, our bass saxophonist, couldn't help but notice my pale, rigid face. Without a word, he handed me a bottle of gin. I tried to tell him I didn't drink but he poured me a glass of gin and said, 'Here, this will stiffen you up. You have to go out there and *sing* now.' So I drank it.

I had no idea then that I was allergic to gin, but I soon found out. Benny was playing 'Skylark' beautifully, and I came staggering out to the microphone. 'Skylark . . . have you anything . . .' Nothing more would come out. I stared at the audience. They stared at me. They laughed. I tried to back up from the microphone, barely able to move. By now they were laughing uproariously, and I was thinking, 'How cruel. How cruel. They don't know about Frank.'

Benny, meanwhile, trying to figure out what was bothering me, just stood with his clarinet at his side, with the reed pointing towards me at about mid-thigh . . . During those days Benny had a stream of dignified gentlemen who would visit him with a briefcase of reeds; he would run a scale on one after another of them. Most of them didn't suit him, so he would promptly flip them into the waste basket. Well, I crashed into the one good reed it had taken him so long to find and smashed it! He put the clarinet to his mouth and tried to play, but, thanks to the ruined reed, it came out in squawks and squeaks. I ran off the stage and hid in the dressing room, sure he would fire me, but he didn't.

His reed was gone and so was my flyer. During the following months, I sent candy and cigarettes and socks and wrote letters but received only one piece of a letter. It said, 'Darling, I'm going to take a chance and tell you more than I should – ' The letter was cut off at that point by the censors. I never heard from him again.

In 1941 the Bobby Soxers were storming the Paramount Theatre in Times Square. I was there with Benny Goodman. Frank Sinatra was the 'Extra Added Attraction', and he certainly was!

We used to lean out the windows of the dressing rooms to see the crowds of swooners, like swarms of bees down there in the street, just waiting for the sight of Sinatra.

It must have been unimaginably exciting for him . . . his days were filled with interviews and autographs and all the things that go with the fireworks of sudden fame, to say nothing of all the performances that could be crowded between newsreels. Everything that led up to Frank's performance seemed not quite so important. Benny played as great as ever, I sang my songs and got a little attention, but it was electric when Frank came out on stage.

One day I was violently ill with the flu. I tried to make every show, but finally I just couldn't. Sinatra discovered I was in my dressing room having a really bad time, and, from that time until I was well, he was my special nurse. He brought me blankets to stop the shivering. Then when it was possible, a little tea; later a piece of toast. Meantime, he was out there singing six or eight shows a day in that huge theatre with the cheering crowds – 'All or Nothing at All', 'I'll Never Smile Again' . . .

Through the years Frank has shown me many other kindnesses. I won't forget those, but I especially remember what he did for me in the middle of his first great triumph: he could have been too busy, but he wasn't.

We were sitting in a café in Passaic, New Jersey, on Sunday 7 December 1941. Well, you all know what we heard from Roosevelt. 'We are at war.' A shudder went through everyone, and it was really hard to go back to the theatre and carry on as though everything was all right.

We started doing bond show after bond show – mostly in Times Square between regular shows, and things became more and more hectic . . . We were playing in Prospect Park in Brooklyn, surrounded by metal bars because the crowds would push up and practically impale themselves. Benny and I had a huge hit record at the time, 'Somebody Else Is Taking My Place', and the crowd sort of went wild when I sang it. It, of course, was right in the mood of the war, and people could especially identify with its theme. They loved hearing Benny do 'Clarinet à la King' and became even more demonstrative when we performed such as 'The Way You Look Tonight', 'Don't Get Around Much Any More' and 'Where or When'. After one show, my gown was ripped off, as Dick Haymes, the male vocalist, and I ran to escape in the subway. A Navy pilot helped us get away. I'm convinced we never would have made it without him.

I stumbled home that night wondering what was next. When I opened the door to the apartment, a wave of heat hit me like a blast furnace. The air was filled with smoke. It turned out to be only the smoke from the fireplaces mixed with the hot humid air. 'A Coke,' I thought. 'I'll get me a Coke!' So in the kitchen I felt something drip on my head – there was a big bulge around the light cord and bulb. My brother Milford had taught me enough about electricity to know that water conducted it. Almost as bad, I looked down at the floor and there were hundreds of ants crawling in and out of the cupboard. I started to whimper like a frightened baby and thought, 'I'd better tell the neighbours upstairs,' so I opened the back door, only to find the steps loaded with our Coca-Cola bottles! I pushed them back a little on each step so I could get outside to call for help, but I missed my footing and came sliding down the steps with ants and broken glass all over me.

Luckily at this point Janie came home with a friend and rescued me. Still bejewelled, but sniffling and scratched, I must have looked very different from the girl who had been singing on the stage only an hour ago, surrounded by fans applauding and asking for autographs.

4

The Man I Love

The day Benny hired guitarist David Barbour, a new life was about to begin for me. We were in Detroit, and I had just come off stage after singing 'These Foolish Things' and was slowly going back over to the iron steps that led upstairs to the dressing room. The notes the guitarist was playing circled around me as I placed one foot on the step, moved back down, turned around and went back to the wings to listen.

David Barbour – almost from the start, the man of my life. I also watched his every move. It was his way not to seem to pay any attention, but when I saw him proudly showing pictures of his little girls to Dick Haymes, I thought I would die, until I learned from Dick they were his sister's children. My feelings for David grew and grew. When I noticed he didn't eat very much, I would fix up his meals at the coffee shop counter in the New Yorker – a little salt and pepper, a little butter, a little coaxing.

When we would go walking, he would sometimes step off the kerb and walk in the street. I just thought he was eccentric. Of course, I would step off and walk with him. The problem of alcoholism never entered my mind. He was so precisely neat and his behaviour was impeccable, plus his wild sense of humour.

But one night he didn't arrive at the usual time, and my stomach was doing flips. I went to his room and found him anything but sober. I ran to the house doctor and asked if he could give me something to sober him up. He mixed something in a bottle and I promptly ran back to David with it. Benny was strict about being prompt and even more so about liquor. The doctor's magic elixir seemed to pull him together, and we got through that one all right, but something told me it would only be a matter of time . . .

At this stage of the war in addition to the bond rallies, we were also playing in hospitals, and soon the band was heading for California. There was a threat of a recording strike, so Benny recorded everything he had in the 'bank'; 'How Deep is the Ocean?' was one of the last ones. We did some sextette numbers – 'Where or When' and 'The Way You Look Tonight' – at the Liederkranz Hall. Benny wanted to use one microphone for the musicians and the singer, which called for gymnastics. Lou McGarrity, playing trombone, would first crawl up in the air (on boxes), then for the vocal we had to pass each other as silently as possible while I crawled *up*, and he *down* for the vocal. Those recordings may sound moody and somehow they were, but it was also a little dangerous – either of us could have crashed to the floor. But if Benny said do it, we did it.

During all the other recordings I found a bench in the restroom and took a little catnap while waiting for my 'Why Don't You Do Right?', which was the very last one. Oh, the glamorous life of a star!

Usually there was little time for sleeping. In New York, besides the Paramount Theatre, we were playing a set in the Terrace Room at the New Yorker Hotel. Popsie, the band boy, used to bring us sandwiches, because they played only newsreels between shows, which didn't leave much time for casual dining, especially for a lady with make-up and hair and all. We worked seven days a week and after several weeks were like those little Swiss toys in a cuckoo clock . . .

One evening my body must have been at an all-time low. I went home to my apartment and fell into bed – make-up, pompadour and all. I could have slept on nails.

The phone rang. I stumbled to it. It was Sam, the doorman at the Paramount. My eyes like saucers, I picked up the receiver. 'Hmmmm?' Sam said, 'Fifteen minutes is in.'

I almost said, 'In where?' but couldn't speak. I turned around a couple of times, grabbed my favourite ensemble – gabardine suit and top coat. No time for stockings. Just shoes. Never mind the hair.

As I stepped into the elevator, people stared at me, and, as soon as I realized the pompadour was listing over one ear, I didn't blame them. I just hoped they didn't also notice I wasn't wearing stockings. It seemed like for ever until we reached the ground floor . . . they never took their eyes off me. I made my escape to the street and caught a cab. 'Paramount Theatre backstage,' I growled, and the cabbie roared away to the theatre.

Sam was holding the door as I streaked through and jumped into the elevator. I thought I heard Benny announcing me, probably did. I slipped into an off-the-shoulder black 'Yukon Lil' gown in about ten seconds. Still didn't touch my hair, ten seconds to slather my face with greasepaint. With hands shaking, I tried the mascara and stuck it in my eye. Then I couldn't see so I stuck my finger in the pot of lipstick and deliberately drew two parallel lines for lips. Still hadn't combed my hair. I quickly chose a big pink French rose and pinned it inside the pompadour. Get the picture?

Now – a dash for the stage. Blessed Sam was holding the elevator for me. I ran across stage as Benny was going into what I would learn was his third announcement. 'And now, ladies and gentlemen, our charming and lovely vocalist, Miss Peggy Lee,' followed by the orchestral introduction.

I burst through the curtain – and the audience laughed. Benny's mouth dropped open, the orchestra snickered, and I thought desperately, 'I'll sing so good they won't pay any attention.' Oh, really?

Every other morning I had to warm up to hit my first note which was C above middle C. The song was 'Don't Get Around Much Anymore'. Well, the first note was terrible, echoing all the way up to the top balcony. The rest of the notes were similar, and the audience was falling apart; the orchestra could no longer play because they were doubled over.

We got through it somehow, and, as Benny stepped to the microphone to announce my second number, I gave him a shove, ran to my dressing room and locked the door.

Why Benny didn't fire me on the spot, I don't know, but I do know he wasn't happy about seeing David and me so happy together.

He gave David his notice, but David stayed with the band for a few weeks, while we all packed up. It was 1943 and we were leaving New York for Los Angeles, where I was to do a film called *The Powers Girl*.

Getting his notice made David realize he loved me and didn't want us to be separated so he *finally* asked me to marry him. I was so excited I couldn't stop grinning. We had our blood tests, got our licence, I bought a lovely dress and we went to City Hall with my sister Marianne and David's best man, Joe Rushton. David had no inclination for big ceremonies. Ours was simple and was conducted by Judge Lilly – a lady judge. We had dinner at Musso-Frank's. I was so in love with David I don't even remember what we ate.

Someone had found us a duplex apartment across the street from the Los Angeles City College. I was so busy decorating and keeping house I wasn't even aware that 'Why Don't You Do Right?' had become a monster hit all over the world – until the telephone started ringing with offers I had never dreamed would come my way.

The telephone in our modest apartment was a stand-up with the receiver hanging on the side. It sat on top of a Chinese red lacquered drop-leaf table. When it rang, I would usually trip over the carpet or the cord, listen to the fabulous offers to play this theatre or that hall and then hear myself say, 'No, thank you, I'm so happy being a housewife.' David thought I was crazy and would often tell me so, but love is a powerful thing, isn't it?

As a newlywed, I was a caution. When the stove caught fire while I was making toast, I would use a North Dakota remedy and pour on generous amounts of salt to kill the flames. David would come out rubbing the sleep from his eyes and say, 'I'm not going to eat that – salt or no salt.'

We would have company, and I was forever making curried this or curried that because it sounded so exotic. Eventually, I curried myself right out. Our first guests were Jess Stacy, a jazz pianist who was going with singer Lee Wiley. They raved about my curry. You couldn't even talk to me after that. I was the curry queen.

Then the doctor told me I was pregnant. I ran all the way home to tell David. I knew I would always cherish what he said when I told him I was pregnant, but I didn't expect what I heard.

'David, we're going to have a baby!'

A long pause then, 'Why, Peg, I hardly know you.'

We were both overjoyed. David's smile lasted throughout the pregnancy.

I had stopped working altogether, Benny Goodman was getting all the royalties from my hits, and until David could get a California union card, he could earn only a pittance in Los Angeles. In order to establish himself with the union, he had to do things way beneath him and worked very late at night, playing at a joint on Skid Row called the Waldorf Cellar. I used to wait up for him, so we would sleep late in the morning. It seems that during my pregnancy, I walked in my sleep and because of the pregnancy could not lie comfortably with any night clothes. One of my sleepwalking episodes that astounded David concerned the iceman. Our little apartment didn't have a refrigerator, just an icebox, and the iceman would bring our big cakes of ice up the stairs, the ice resting on a thick rubber pad on his back with the water melting behind him. The man was not a teetotaller and one day failed to come – he had probably taken a day off to get drunk – and as a result, our rationed food spoiled. I resolved to find another iceman, and the thought evidently stuck in my subconscious.

The next morning I was dreaming and, while sound asleep, went walking around the apartment in the nude as I wound the alarm clock. I set the clock for 2.00 p.m. – why I picked that hour I don't know. Suddenly the iceman appeared in front of me, looked at me, horrified, and tried to back *down* the steps, repeating rapidly, 'Yesma'amyesma'amyesma'am . . .'

I said, 'We won't be needing you anymore,' and walked into the kitchen and placed the alarm clock on the icebox. End of dream. I slept on until I heard the alarm and got up to find it in the kitchen on top of the icebox set for 2.00 p.m.

The iceman never returned!

I told the obstetrician about the sleepwalking, and he told us to tie one of my legs to the end of the bed. We did that, but, after the iceman, sometimes I would have an awful time trying to convince David I was awake.

We named our little girl after grandfather Nicholas. I wanted to call her Nicole, but Nicki won out.

I had to have some special medical attention at the beginning, because it seemed I had two large tumours. When Nicki was born, I really found out how much David loved me, as if I didn't know before. She was an eight-month Caesarean, and I had pneumonia. David was so frightened – my chances seemed alarmingly slim.

They gave me a spinal, so I could hear everything he and they said, including the doctor running alongside the gurney and telling the nurses, 'Find my damn shoes, find them now!' and the nurse saying, 'Where are the beads? Where are the beads?' I thought they were looking for a rosary instead of an identification bracelet.

David called my beloved Marianne, and cried and said, 'I'll never do that to her again.' We both wanted more children, but that wasn't to be possible.

When they wheeled me back into my room, I looked happily at the picture of some pansies at the end of my bed and said to my nurse, 'Don't they have dear little faces?' She thought I was delirious and was seeing babies, so they put up the bars on my bed and replaced the pansies with a picture of a smiling baby.

71

Nicki turned out to be beautiful and healthy and very early showed signs of high intelligence. David was, as you might guess, mad about her. She learned to laugh early and loved to rock her high chair until it started to tip. I would run and slide in as though to first base, and she would fall on me, and both of us would laugh and laugh.

Eventually I was lured out of my housekeeping job. Perhaps because of the jazz sound of 'Why Don't You Do Right?', Dave Dexter saw the potential of a jazz singer in my voice. For whatever reason, he asked if I would come down and record a couple of songs for an album called *New American Jazz* – 'Ain't Goin' No Place' and 'That Old Feeling'. I still love that song. Eddie Miller played a classic saxophone solo on 'That Old Feeling'. It was fun to sing again, but at that time it didn't mean as much to me as staying home and keeping house.

The record was a success, and soon a lot of people thought I should go out again, including David, who may or may not have been influenced by Carlos Gastel. David's argument was by far the most interesting to me – use the talent given to me rather than later resent that I hadn't. I really didn't have enough self-esteem going for me – the scars of my childhood weren't yet healed.

The next step was meeting Carlos, a formidable manager, who handled such stars as Stan Kenton, Woody Herman, June Christy, Mel Torme and Nat King Cole. A large, very pleasant fellow with a great sense of humour, he introduced me to one of the finest agents ever – Tom Rockwell, founder of General Artists Corporation and discoverer of a list of star talents that included the Mills Brothers, Perry Como, Dinah Shore . . . To him each talent was like a jewel for which he provided the setting.

There was another agent on the grand scale, Levis Green, who had plans for me to replace Lana Turner who, I was told, wanted out of her studio. In the end it was Ava Gardner who wore the crown. I turned it down, which, looking back, may or may not have been imprudent. All I wanted to do was to stay home and be a housewife and a mother.

The songs on *New American Jazz* made a pleasant debut, and what a thrill to turn on the radio and hear DJs Al Jarvis and Gene Norman play 'That Old Feeling' and 'Ain't Goin' No Place'. Suddenly I was meeting people such as Buddy De Sylva, Glenn

Wallichs and Johnny Mercer (who together founded Capitol Records). Sy Devore was the leading tailor of the day, and those fellows were conducting business upstairs over Sy's tailor shop on Vine, just below Sunset. Little did we all know that that was the beginning of the large round Capitol Building on Vine as it stands today.

At one of those meetings over Sy Devore's shop, it was decided that David and I would record for Capitol, and the subject of material or songs came up for discussion. While I'd been pregnant with Nicki, I had begun to write ideas for songs. For instance, one day several things happened that delighted me. Someone brought us a pheasant, another person brought over a bottle of fine wine, the telephone was full of nice messages – some of those offers I mentioned – and finally I said to no one in particular, 'Well, it's a good day!' Which struck me as a good title. As I busied myself with housework, I began to sing a little 'dummy' melody, and the words kept popping in, so I lay down the vacuum or whatever and wrote them down. When it was finished, I practically ran down to my sister's apartment house, called up to her window and sang the song. She always took great pride in having been the first person to hear 'It's a Good Day!'.

When David came home, I couldn't wait to sing it to him. He then took out some manuscripts and worked out the harmonies for what was to be our first big hit.

'What More Can a Woman Do?' was also inspired by my feelings for David and our life. I was washing dishes, and just sang out my love for him . . . So, that's how these things happened, and it was Johnny Mercer who felt the songs had strong potential. He was right. When I was working on 'I Don't Know Enough About You', he made some wonderfully constructive comments. He advised me to tear it all apart and do it over again. It really was fun reconstructing it, and it was a vast improvement. That was probably one of my best instructions on construction – by a master.

We were often invited to Carlos Gastel's home. (Carlos was managing both David and me now.) His wife Joan had to be the soul of patience, because life was one big party, or one big martini, for Carlos.

He had a very nice boat that was called a 'stinkpot' by the more refined sailors who only had sails and a small auxiliary motor for emergencies. Some of them, although they couldn't help but like

Carlos, would look down their noses at him because he drove his boat like a truck-driver who had imbibed generously.

I'm sure Carlos didn't have to pour it down his throat, but he was a bad influence on David. David's favourite was a boilermaker – bourbon and beer. The beer always looked so harmless by itself. (He even fed the goldfish bourbon!) I think one of the main reasons I would go boating with them was to maintain some sanity . . . David liked to play marlin: he would jump in the ocean, and I would have to reel him in like a marlin.

We had all the usual domestic crises in our household but never any quarrelling between David and myself. There was some playful pushing if he was drinking, but mostly he had a lovely quiet disposition. I did too. I wish I had it now. The years of things being difficult finally hardened up the edges a bit, increasing my already overdeveloped sense of responsibility. And I was exceedingly neurotic about Nicki. I didn't sleep, listening and watching her all night long.

It was at this point that Ernest Holmes, founder of Science of Mind, came into my life. My early experiences with organized religion had not been exactly positive. My first minister, when I was a child in North Dakota, had been a Nazi, literally, a member of the Bund. It wasn't until I met Ernest Holmes that I realized that we live in a universe that is primarily spiritual, and that it is possible to get everything we need – health, money, happiness – through the scientific application of prayer and meditation.

David and I had a neighbour named Honey Frambach. One day she knocked on my door, introduced herself, and I invited her in for a chat.

'I never see you go out,' Honey said.

'We can't afford it, to tell you the truth.' (It was true at the time, with me being a homebody, wife and mother, and David struggling.)

The subject of spiritual beliefs somehow came up, and she asked me if I'd heard of Ernest Holmes, then told me about some of his ideas.

'He sounds wonderful,' I said. 'I'd love to hear him.'

She volunteered to take care of Nicki if I wanted to go hear Dr Holmes speak, and a short time later I went to his institute at Sixth and Vernon in Los Angeles. I was the first one to arrive, and as I sat in the lecture hall I noticed a small brass plaque with a name on it on the chair in front of me. Curious, I circled around to see whose name was on the back of the chair I had selected – it read 'Estelle Frambach'. Listening to Dr Holmes, I thought I had, indeed, found something I could seriously relate to in Science of Mind. I have never stopped in that conviction.

About this time I went back east to substitute for Jo Stafford on the 'Chesterfield Supper Club' radio show. When I arrived in New York, I had such stomach flu I couldn't even drink water. Carlos had to sit in my suite, because I couldn't be alone. On the day of the show, I couldn't get out of bed. Carlos rang Dr Palmer, who came over, took a look at me and said, 'You can't make it, it would be unwise for you to even try.'

I wasn't convinced. How could I fly all the way from California – it was a very big deal in the day of prop planes – and not do this show? I called Ernest Holmes in Los Angeles and explained my predicament.

'Just lie back down and rest for a minute,' he said, then told me to affirm the omnipresence of God, and the omniscience of God, who knows what needs to be done. Affirm, too, his omnipotence – nothing is impossible to God. Finally, Ernest stressed the value of being grateful and of giving thanks.

It worked, I got well enough and went on for Jo Stafford and did the show. When I told Ernest Holmes about this, he said, 'Please come and see me when you get back to LA.' I did, and it was the beginning of a lifelong friendship.

When Nicki became ill I ran to Ernest Holmes and poured out my heart to him. 'Peggy,' he said, 'you're going to make that child really sick by your constant worry. You must learn to trust, to have faith. You and I will do some work for her right now, and you'll see that she is all right.' We did, and she was fine. She was so precious to me, and I knew she would be our only child, so I really had to overhaul my thinking. With Ernest Holmes' help, I did.

It was about that time that David's mother, Bessie, came out from the East to live with us, and our life changed. I nervously tried to make everything as perfect as I could for her, and then David sprung one on me: 'Peg, I'm working at the studio when my mother gets here, so I want you to go down to Union Station and meet her.'

Meet her? Find her! I have no sense of direction, but I was pretty good at street car tracks, so I finally figured out how I would take the red car down to Union Station and really splurge and bring her home in a cab. When I think of that now, it's hysterical. Miss Capable was a complete failure at finding places . . .

'David,' I said, 'I've never even met her. I want to welcome her *here*.'

'Oh, you can welcome her there.'

I might have sensed there was something strained in their relationship, but I didn't then. Well, I got up in the middle of the night, checked the apartment, did the washing, made some food for lunch, got myself dressed after giving David his breakfast and met Honey Frambach, my neighbour, who was going to watch Nicki while I went to pick up Bessie. 'Cause 'I'm a Woman, W-O-M-A-N!'

My sisters and I had looked for a little apartment for Bessie that David and I could afford and that was close to us and comfortable. Della, Marianne and I painted the little place, put up curtains, some of David's and my prints for the walls, did everything we could to make it liveable.

When we got back from the station, we proudly took her downstairs, and she promptly refused to stay alone on the ground floor. So my little dining room became her bedroom with a folding bed.

No doubt Bessie found it difficult to give up her 'Sonny', as she called David – he was definitely not a 'Sonny'. David had given up drinking when we married, but now he took up his old hobby again. I learned then that he had had a problem with alcohol before we met, which explained the little incidents when we were with Benny.

Meanwhile, I had been working outside of home as well as in. By the time the season was over, my health was in a bad way – I had a white-cell count of 17,000, which indicates a severe infection. When he got it down a bit, the doctor wanted to send me to Palm Springs to completely rest and soak up the sunshine. David asked Bessie if she would go down with Nicki and me, and she agreed to go – for a fee! This, when we were supporting her.

Well, we went, but I might as well have been alone. After that I gave up my dream of adopting her as a mother. I did come to love David's father, though. He was a fine gentleman.

Now the recordings began in earnest at Capitol. From the start you could tell that either they were doing a great job of promoting, or we had a lot of genuine hits. Well, both were true, and offers *really* began flooding in.

And in the midst of it all one fateful thing happened whose

significance I didn't even realize. Benny convinced David and me that I should go to the Golden Gate Theatre in San Francisco and play with him there for one week. A young Navy fighter pilot, Dewey Martin, came into the theatre and decided he would marry me (and years later, he *did*). But at the time David and I were a devoted couple, and for me the pilot was just a member of the audience.

But these personal appearances did create tensions, and other things began to gnaw away at us – David and Carlos were bar buddies, which I can understand in a way. They made each other laugh and laugh, not realizing they both had an alcoholic problem.

At parties a lot of our friends thought I was being a possessive wife because I was always urging that we go home. The real reason was that I could tell when David had reached the danger point; they, on the outside, couldn't see it.

I remember one time we were driving home. 'David,' I said, 'there's a police car just ahead, be careful.' 'Yes? OK, I'll catch him,' said David, and put his foot on the gas pedal! I don't know how we missed that one, but we arrived home safely without doing anyone any harm . . . Except, of course, the drinking *was* doing harm, because by now David was showing signs of ulcers. I had him on a strict diet, but it didn't help much with the bourbon chaser.

Building our first dream house on Blair Drive in the Hollywood Hills did seem to make him happy, though. He came home one day wearing a plaid lumber jacket and work shoes and proudly announced, 'Well, we broke ground today!' I really cracked up, because it was so unlike the impeccably dressed man I knew who wore tweed jackets and birdseye shirts with a rather thin black knit tie. Sometimes cashmere pullovers. He was thin, with brown eyes, Italian eyes, kind of a shy smile, and a magnificent face. I used to think he was a cross between Cary Grant, Abraham Lincoln and Jesus. If he felt especially affectionate, he'd call me 'Dolly' or 'Normer'. And he had a wonderfully dry sense of humour.

Our songs were Duke Ellington's 'Perdido' and 'Warm Valley'. 'Chelsea Bridge' wasn't bad either. I got so carried away listening to that one day, I poured salt instead of sugar into the apple pie I was making to surprise him.

We made trips day after day to the house and supervised every detail. How we loved it! Each time we would say to Nicki, 'We're going up to see Nicki's house.' When we were there, we would say, 'This is Nicki's bedroom, this is Nicki's bathroom . . .'

Eventually the day arrived when the house was finished. I was doing some last-minute packing, having bathed and dressed Nicki, and was babbling about taking Nicki to her brand new home. She looked so sad that finally I said, 'What's the matter, honey, aren't you happy that we're going to your new house?' She began to cry and sobbed, 'Do I have to live there all alone?'

When we moved in we were just like any other perfect couple who had built their first dream house. The landscaping had been completed, but they had left us just enough room to put in some bedding plants around the patio so we could play in our own soil.

By now I was singing with Bing Crosby on the 'Kraft Music Hall' and Jimmy Durante on his Rexall programme – not one, but two of the greatest entertainers that ever lived – and I had the pleasure of going to the NBC and CBS studios and working with them. I became a 'regular', and every week there was a parade of stars: Judy Garland, Oscar Levant, Tallulah Bankhead, Claudette Colbert, Greer Garson, Margaret O'Brien, Zsa Zsa Gabor, Charles Boyer and George Sanders. Working two networks simultaneously, I guess I met just about everyone in radio in those days.

We had found a marvellous housekeeper and a nurse for Nicki. Martina Garberg and dear Alice Larson were the most efficient, capable, loving people one could ask for. They would take turns travelling with us or taking care of Nicki. It was absolute heaven! Our house was filled with music and laughter. All we needed to complete this picture of wedded bliss was a pet – a dog.

One day a stray came up out of the Warner Brothers hills, dragging her poor hind legs, with a film over her eyes so she could barely see. David and I brought her inside and gave her a bit of nourishment before we took her to the veterinarian. He didn't hold too much hope for her, but we were determined to try. With special care and time, she got her dear self back together.

I don't know why, but David named her 'Banjo'. Maybe he wasn't sure she was a she; he never was much for animal husbandry. Finally, she was home again and what a lovely surprise to see the beautiful coat of fur growing, and the soulful eyes.

During this time, *Life* magazine did a photo layout on us and Banjo was in the background of one of the pictures. Well, as fate would have it, Frank Weatherwax, the world-famous trainer, saw the picture and recognized our dog as one of the offspring of his famous 'Lassie'. One day he drove by our house and saw Banjo cavorting in the front garden. Not knowing what had taken place, he set some wheels in motion that had a fairly profound effect on several people.

I was in Chicago headlining in the Chicago Theatre when the Chicago *Tribune* or *Sun-Times* ran the big black headline 'PEGGY LEE STEALS DOG!' The phone rang off the hook with calls from the press asking me if it was true. Had I really stolen a dog? The story went on to say the dog was sired by 'Lassie' and that I would be sued for one million dollars for ruining the dog's education (and that was before inflation).

I indignantly made a statement: 'If befriending a starving animal is a crime, I am guilty!' And how could they sue me? How could I know the animal had such an extraordinary education? Scandalized though I was, I did feel rather important having such a big headline.

When I called home I got another shock. The former owner had found our house, walked into our garden and told our gardener he was taking Banjo. 'How did Banjo react?' I asked. 'Was she glad to see him?' My gardener assured me that she had shown dislike and fear, so I decided to fight for her.

We had our business managers, George Stuart and Dick Shipman, and our lawyers do some investigating and learned that the previous owner had worked for Frank Weatherwax as a trainer. He had been given Banjo (who had been named 'Lady') but she had run away – to us, and was our beloved pet for many, many years.

As I said, I was appearing with Crosby and Durante, and once, when Jimmy was ill, I helped act as hostess. The marvellous Frank Morgan (the Wizard of Oz) was the star guest host. Jackie Burnett had written a successful production number, 'Any State in the 48 is Great', which was fairly complicated, especially for those not used to singing.

After dress rehearsal, Frank decided to fortify himself with something from the bar across the street. I was getting nervous because the announcer was warming up the audience for the live show, which was to begin in minutes. At the last moment Mr Morgan walked in with a big smile on his face. Seeing my look of panic, he said kindly, 'Stick with me, kid. I'll get you in plenty of trouble.'

Actually, it was a very funny show, including Victor Moore getting his foot caught in a tin can dropped by the sound effects man and clanking his way to the microphone to sing with Frank Morgan, Arthur Treacher, and yours truly . . .

Those were the days, my friend.

I used to call Durante, Mr Love. It seemed to me he was all love. He once said to me, 'Someday you will feel something come back to you from the audience and then you won't ever feel afraid again.'

Life was so beautiful and happy that I began to be afraid it wouldn't last. And it didn't. David was having more and more pain in his stomach until, finally, we had to get him to another doctor for a second opinion.

A decision had to be made about the bleeding duodenal ulcers. Diet hadn't worked, it became acute, and we rushed him to St John's Hospital where Dr Arnold Stevens, his surgeon, operated on him.

It seemed like for ever before I saw Dr Stevens again, and I ran to meet him. He wasn't smiling. 'I think he's going to make it, but it's about a fifty-fifty chance. We had to remove about three fourths of his stomach, and he's lost a lot of blood.'

'But he *is* going to live . . . isn't he?'

'We've done all we can do. It's in God's hands.'

For twelve days and nights I sat in the little waiting area near David's room, making frequent trips in to see him. During those times we talked of love, and he promised to hang on. He asked me not to let his mother in the room because she made him nervous. That put me in a difficult position, but my vows were to him, so I kept them. At least until he was out of the danger zone.

Whenever I could be certain he would be all right for an hour or two, I would dash home for a shower and a change of clothes. Nicki, with Martina's help, would pick a camellia from the bushes in front of our house to take to her daddy as a reminder that he'd better get well and come home.

His humour saw me through on several occasions. When they were wheeling him to the operating room for the second surgery, I ran alongside the gurney trying to think of something to say, but all I could think of was, 'I love you, David, I love you.' He looked at me through the tubes and oxygen and said, 'Stop nagging me.'

I was in constant touch with Ernest Holmes, and am convinced that without the power of affirmative prayer, David would not have survived. In affirmative prayer you don't just say please give me something; you state the fact that as a child of God you are entitled to your birthright, your abundance. I also became close friends with the nuns and the priests. They were faithful throughout and, incidentally, have remained so. (One of the young priests is now the head of a large Trappist monastery, and we have kept in touch.) Even the girls who washed the halls were so thoughtful, putting cloths down on the wet floor so I could make my trips to see David without interruption. I think everyone in that hospital had David on their mind and in their hearts. Regular bulletins were given on the radio. Everyone was so thoughtful and loving.

After a few more scares, our prayers were answered, and he came around. It was wonderful to see how friends gathered and lent their support. Then, about the ninth day, David said, 'Honey, why don't you at least go out and have dinner? I'm so much better today, and you should do that. Will you, please? Just a little more, and I'll be fine.' I agreed, and we went to a restaurant nearby. I was edgy and reached a point of nervousness that had me baffled. I kept feeling that I *must* get back to the hospital, so back we went.

When I got in the elevator, I met Doctor Davis. Far from his usual pleasant self, he didn't speak to me. I froze. It was obvious something was terribly wrong. The elevator door opened, there was a high-tension bustle going on, the sisters running this way and that, wheeling a resuscitator into David's room. I tried to get in, but they didn't allow me. Sister Ann Raymond tried to comfort me.

I shall never forget this: as I walked down the corridor crying out to God in silence, I suddenly saw a shaft of light coming from my own eyes down the length of the hall, and I *knew* David was alive and would live. I felt as though I had been lifted from the floor.

'I will set him on high, because he hath known my name' (Psalm 91:14).

I ran back to tell Sister Ann Raymond. At first she thought I was just hysterical or in shock, but as I was saying, 'You don't understand, Sister. I *know* he's all right,' everyone came out of David's room declaring it had been a miracle. He had been blind, now he could see. His heart had stopped, now it was beating normally. All his vital signs were perfect.

'Just a little more, and I'll be fine,' he had said. Who said that?

Three days later they discharged David from the hospital. Praise the Lord!

Both Jimmy Durante and Bing Crosby were among the hundreds of friends who cared so much about David. Bing used to call every morning at six o'clock to see how David was doing.

To celebrate David's recovery, we packed our luggage and ourselves into our convertible and drove to the Rosarita Beach Hotel, down between Tijuana and Ensenada.

It was the first time I'd ever been across the border, and it was fascinating. After all the stress we had been under, it was perfect. The totally relaxed attitude of the people was just what we needed after the hospital. We had to leave our little Nicki at home with Martina, but it was for a good cause: to get David out of the ulcer world.

The happy, relaxed spirit of the place inspired me – you may have guessed it – to write the song 'Mañana'. David got his guitar out, and we had so much fun putting it all together. Of course, we had no idea it would be such a tremendous hit. I remember when we recorded it how contagious the happiness was. Carmen Miranda's 'Brazilians', and her musicians, added a lot with their effervescent samba rhythm. Carmen was often a guest with Durante, and she had called me about using them. She also recommended classical guitarist Laurindo Almeida, who played with me for quite a while. What a dear lady Carmen was, and the Brazilians were perfect for 'Mañana'. When we were doing what I believe was the first 'board fade' (turning down the volume on the studio recording equipment), the Brazilians decided to samba out of the studio and down the street, playing and singing 'Mañana, mañana, mañana is soon enough for me!'

We took the acetate home and played it constantly, it was almost like being a child on Christmas morning to wake up, dash out to the turntable and play it over and over again – doing the samba in my robe!

The record's sales jumped into the millions so fast you couldn't turn on the radio without hearing it – and then one day we were served with papers for a three-million-dollar lawsuit from a banjo player named Hats McKay. I don't know how many millions that would be today! It was what is known as a nuisance suit – I guess you could say a few million could be a nuisance.

We found an excellent attorney, Henry Gilbert, who was Irving Berlin's representative at the time, and there followed months and months of depositions and meetings, including some colourful trivia: H. Edna Moon, a retired violinist and World War I acquaintance of Hats, testified that he wrote the song in 1919. There was also Ginger Lee (no relation), who was the mistress of ceremonies at the Tropics Club in Imperial, California, in 1943. She said, 'Hats sang his "Laughing Song" there. He wore a hula skirt and tin plates for breasts.'

As the trial date approached, Mr Gilbert asked us to keep a large opening in our bookings and arrange to be in New York for the trial so we went to New York and stayed at the Warwick Hotel.

David disappeared. Several days passed. It was impossible not to worry. I wore paths in the carpet of our suite, called every musician's hang-out I could think of. No luck. If anyone had seen him, they weren't going to tell me. He came back almost sober the day before the trial.

When the trial began, Hats was on the stand constantly one-fingering 'Mañana'. It annoyed the judge. 'Do you have to keep playing that thing?' he said.

The lawyer had lined up some impressive experts to testify on our behalf – Deems Taylor, the president of ASCAP (American Society of Composers, Artists and Publishers); Dr Sigmund Spaeth, musical historian and tune detective; Dr Charles Kettering, head curator of the Edison Foundation; and Albert Osbourne who was the handwriting expert at the Hauptmann–Lindbergh trial. So dignified and learned compared with the clown-like little man who had dreamed up this expensive scheme.

I sat next to Deems Taylor. During an intermission, he related a story about himself. He was giving a eulogy at a memorial service for Jerome Kern and, feeling the atmosphere was charged with serious gloom, he ventured to say something warm and less formal. He succeeded all right. He said, 'I've always been a great Fern can myself.'

Meanwhile the serious trial went on and on. Deems Taylor pointed out that it should be 'painfully apparent' that when McKay performed the song, he never repeated the melody the same way (even with one finger). Dr Kettering testified that there were many 'public domain' resemblances to songs such as Vesta Victoria's 'Now I Have to Call Him Father', 'Jo Jo's Laughing Song' or 'If You Had the Brains Your Mother Had'. Mr Albert Osbourne said that, after careful examination, in his opinion the manuscript of Hats McKay's song was made with new ink on new paper.

At this point Judge Wasservogel motioned to me and said, 'There's a phone call for you in my chambers.' I quickly tiptoed in and the voice on the phone said, 'What did dey do to my goil?'

Before we knew it, in came Jimmy Durante followed by Eddie Jackson and Jack Roth. There was a little bedlam in the courtroom while they placed an upright piano near the judge, but he didn't seem to mind.

Jimmy began playing and singing his 'Laughing Song', explaining that every comedian had at least one. They would play and sing the 'Laughing Song', tell a joke and then vamp while the audience laughed. It was usually notated with the words 'ha ha ha' – exactly what Hats McKay had for the lyric to his version of 'Mañana'. Jimmy's testimony certainly bore out the public-domain argument as well as giving us all a laugh and releasing the tension of the courtroom. I wish they could have stayed on, and I suspect the judge wouldn't have minded either.

When we took a recess, I tried to thank Jimmy, but he just shook his famous nose at me and said, 'Dat's what friends are for.' I wanted to cry as I watched them walk down the hallway and out the door.

Sigmund Spaeth's evidence proved our point beyond a shadow of a doubt. Hats McKay's tune was very professionally and clearly marked as a samba. Well, it happens the Brazilian Samba was not in existence in 1919, when Hats claimed he wrote it. We won the case.

Deems Taylor took me to dinner at the Stork Club to celebrate (David didn't want to go, he'd been drinking). We went into the 'leather-bound' Cub Room, and he showed me a leather-bound wine list, which intimidated me, to say the least. Unable to recognize one wine from another, I showed my exquisite sophistication by saying, 'I believe I'll just have some Chianti.'

Deems, stifling a laugh, couldn't resist adding, 'And I suppose for dessert you'd like some cornstarch pudding?'

Dr Stevens, the surgeon who had done such fine work with David, became a good friend, as did the whole family – his wife, Jeanne, their daughters, Carol and Harley, and young Steve.

There was a French Normandy house next to the Stevens' house in Denslow, Westwood Hills, Los Angeles. They say houses reach out and claim you, and that one did just that. I asked Jeanne if she thought the house would ever be for sale.

'No,' she said, 'I don't think they'd ever sell that house. They built it, you know. They chose the hand-hewn beams, the three fireplaces were all personally designed . . .'

'Well, just in case, if they ever do, please let me know. Wouldn't it be nice to be neighbours?' I didn't really think it would be ours, but then you never know, and in a way it did seem to belong to us . . .

Well, one day Jeanne called: 'Did you put a spell on that house? It's for *sale*.'

We got right into the business of buying it and moving in as soon as possible. The morning the moving van came up to Blair Drive and started moving our sentimental things out of our first home, we got a little misty. David and I had had it built and we loved it. We loved our neighbours, too. In fact, our friends, the Joviens, closed all their blinds that day so they wouldn't see the moving van go by.

Decorating was a massive job. This was a large house and we started with a tremendous roll of hand-woven carpeting from China, the last shipment out before the closed-door policy that has lasted all these years. I handpainted all of the cupboards in the kitchen area with pictures of Frenchmen in red berets. Someone told me later that the doors were sold separately. The cupboards were labelled in French and I made only one mistake: *fleur* instead of *farine*, but it looked pretty so we left it there.

(I had always wanted to learn to speak French – when I was a little girl in North Dakota I took books from the library and tried to teach myself. North Dakota, with its heavy Nordic population, was not exactly the place to practise French. Over the years the dream to go to France continued, so it wasn't surprising that I wanted Nicki to learn to speak French. At Westlake School for Girls she turned out to be a good student, but Madam Egan was very firm with her and Nicki had to be talked into continuing every year. I even promised her a little sister . . . from France, and did adopt a little girl through a foster plan. I promised to take her to France, too. We went, much later, but only to the Riviera.)

The house was finally completed and we left to go on tour. Our first stop was Virginia Beach. The stage faced the ocean, and even though the surf was pounding gently on this beautiful balmy evening, it made enough sound to cover a soft musical note. (It seems I'm always listening for a note.) Ray Anthony was conducting his orchestra while David played. Gil Evans, one of the most gifted of all arrangers, was trying to cue me in to 'Where or When'. Twice the ocean breeze blew the note away.

What a setting. The moon, the darkening sky, the ocean, the music of Rogers and Hart . . . Finally, on the third cue, I began to sing . . . And from out of all this loveliness came a bug as big as a hummingbird, drawn by the spotlight to circle around and around my head. 'It seems we . . .' I sang, but the bug had everyone's attention. There wasn't a chance my eyes would stop rolling. I continued to sing, but keeping my mouth closed as much as possible. Try singing 'Where or When' that way.

The audience was fascinated. With all the chivalry he could muster, Ray picked up a giant stack of his music and hit me right on the head. WHAP. The bug was gone, and so was the music.

The musicians started laughing, and as soon as I recovered from the blow, I started to laugh hysterically. The audience followed suit. We had to stop the performance. My make-up was washed away with the tears. Finally, after a couple of unsuccessful attempts, we managed to finish the programme.

We took Nicki along on that trip and we had a wonderful time, but it wasn't enough to keep David on the straight and narrow. We came home to Denslow tired and troubled.

By now my work with Bing and Durante was going full force, and my love for both of them brightened my life. Years earlier I had literally saved pennies to go to see Bing's movies. Tears rolled down my cheeks if the leading lady didn't treat him right. In the film *Mississippi* I was emotionally spent when Bing, brokenhearted, sang 'Down by the River'.

Through the years I sang on Bing's programme, I met the most fantastic stars, like Al Jolson, whom I sang with. Bing was always finding ways to help give me confidence. In fact everyone connected with him was funny and nice and talented.

His nationwide show was live for the East Coast and recorded for the West, so the musicians couldn't afford to be late, but Bing and I were always the first to arrive for rehearsals. I was always impressed by his promptness, his honesty, and his modesty. I remember him saying, 'I wish I could really make something of my life . . .' It amazed me that he could feel so humble. I tried, in a stumbling sort of way, to tell him what the world thought of him, but I don't think I convinced him.

Sometimes he liked to tease me. When he'd find me at the piano, he'd say, 'Hello, Peg. Who are you today? Chopin or Stravinsky?'

'Oh, hello, Bing.' And I would quickly sweep off the piano bench. I never wanted anyone to hear me play, or should I say, hear me *not* play.

One evening in San Francisco, Bing asked me to go to dinner with him, and knowing how prompt he always was, I started to wash my long blonde hair very early. It was a fairy-tale situation, my idol actually asking me for a date!

Make-up and hair finished early, I eagerly awaited the sound of the doorbell. When it finally rang, I thought, 'I'll just spray a little of this hair spray to make sure . . .'

It was the wrong can, it was sweet-scented room deodorizer! I turned all colours and Bing laughed and laughed as I tried everything, and finally ended up washing my reeking hair.

He took me to one of San Francisco's great restaurants and during dinner I told him about how I had felt about his movies. Then we cruised all over that wonderful city until we found a pianist who could play 'Down by the River' in Bing's key, and he sang to me at our table. The tears rolled again.

He used to write little funny notes, which I would find in my mailbox upon arrival at some city. It meant so much, especially out there on the road, to hear from someone like Bing. Once he sent me a wire referring to his last appearance at the Coconut Grove. It seems he had 'hit the sauce' a little there; his wire said, 'Dear Peg, please pick up my laundry. I left there rather hurriedly in 1931. Love, Bing.'

Bing also gave me the loveliest painting by Busquets, a modern primitive of Paris that inspired me to write this lyric, which Paul Horner set to music:

Petit Chanson de Rêves
I long to go to France because I want to see
The things I've only read about of gay Paree

I want to hear where music came to Debussy
And that would touch the very heart
And soul of me
The Louvre museum, the gardens of the Tuileries
La Rue Pigalle where painters paint
The things they see
And we may find a Renoir or a Claude Monet
A painting that would surely take my breath away
On top of old Montmartre the dome of Sacre Coeur
Where the view is endless and the air is pure
To see the palace of Versailles aglow with light
Then stroll beside the Seine upon a summer night
To fall in love with someone in a quaint café
To walk the city streets until the break of day
To fall so much in love that I might want to stay
To know my heart will break when I must go away
Little song of my dreams
Petit chanson de rêves

I've been as near as De Gaulle and Orly airports, but I've never been *in* Paris. Each year I plan to go, but maybe I'll just sing the song . . .

Bing was always so protective and so sensitive during my early days of nerves and selfconsciousness. Just before air time on one of my first Kraft programmes, he found me standing rigid outside the studio at NBC and asked what he could do to help. I managed to say, 'When you introduce me, would you please not leave me out there on the stage alone? Would you stand where I can see your feet?' From then on he always casually leant on a speaker or piano to give me the support I needed to learn about being at ease on stage.

You have to love a man like that. He offered everything – money, cars, his own blood, and even volunteered to babysit with our little daughter, Nicki, while David was so sick in hospital.

The last time I saw Bing we were both doing a benefit performance. It was beautiful, if brief. He called to me, 'Hello, baby! So good to see you.' I was grateful I got to see him one more time.

Yes, once we walked along, Bing – down by the river.

* * *

Jimmy Van Heusen is a wonderful man. I've heard many a song of his in its growing stages because David and I used to stay at his house in Palm Springs a lot, and he was always around the Crosby Show. Bing did so many of his songs. His partner, Johnny Burke, was a great lyricist, as, of course, is Sammy Cahn.

Once when Jimmy was doing some writing for a Crosby show, we were at the St Francis Hotel in San Francisco and somehow we got lost in the bowels of the building – we had been rehearsing in a dining room and took the wrong door. We were bent over under the pipes and came to a sliding door. You could look right down into the kitchen. If we had taken a few more steps, we would have fallen into it. We finally did get out, and Jimmy and I sat on a kerbstone, à la Alec Wilder, and had a long conversation. You know how the houses are in San Francisco. If you opened the window in your house, you would be right out on the kerb. We were talking away, and the people opened the window and said if we didn't stop that and get out of there, they would have us arrested for loitering.

Jimmy was on the tall side, and he didn't have a lot of hair. Somewhere I've read that men who are bald are very virile – you've heard that. Jolly blue eyes and enormously attractive to women. Oh, yes, he had a lot of women crazy about him. Jimmy was a very good friend.

David and I had some radio programmes for a while, sponsored by Rexall and Oldsmobile, and I did a lot of guest spots. In other words, I was *very* busy. Sometimes we would bring the whole cast home for spaghetti or chilli – David would invite them, I would cook, and then he would come and say, 'Get rid of these people.'

The pressure of all this began to tell on David; at the last minute before we were due to go on tour Dr Stevens and my manager, Carlos, told me that David was not emotionally fit to go, that I would have to go my myself. David's drinking was totally out of hand, so I took off for St Louis solo. (It wasn't too easy on my health either. I came home from this tour with pneumonia.)

Opening day, the orchestra leader, Griff Williams, came out to rehearse with, basically, tenor saxophones. My arrangements were for a different instrumentation and I suddenly realized no one had made any provisions for that – what I found in the music trunk were parts for trumpets, trombones, flutes, strings. No saxophones.

I was learning the hard way. One call to our librarian from Dave or Carlos could have prevented this. Griff, who was so drunk he introduced me that opening night as Susan Reed, was of no help. I meditated. I called Ernest Holmes. 'You don't have time to feel sorry for yourself,' he said, 'just put it together and do it. I'll work for you, too.'

As if in answer, Mike Bryant, a fine jazz guitarist, called out of the blue. 'How are you?' I said, 'Come down here and bring your guitar.' He said, 'I don't have one. I gave it away.' I said, 'Find one and bring a bass player, too.'

I had brought Sid Hurwitz and Billy Exiner, who had played with Tony Bennett and Claude Thornhill. Bryant turned up with a bass player, a very good one. We simply picked out seventeen tunes, all standards – Gershwin, Porter, Arlen, Rogers and Hart, Kern – tunes that have served me throughout my career, to play with the quartet.

But Harold Kopler, the boss man, protested. He thought that if you hire Peggy Lee you also got David Barbour. He didn't want to let me go on, said he would close the room. I had invited twelve little blind children from a local school to enjoy the show. Now what was I going to tell them? They had been so excited about the invitation.

Then the union people started to look tough. They said to Kopler, 'If you're not going to honour your contract, we're going to close down your chain.' That meant a lot of people would be out of work.

I called Carlos, who said, 'Well, you're really in trouble.' You notice – *he* wasn't, *I* was. I quietly went to my room. Kopler was saying, 'No David Barbour, no engagement.' The union was saying, 'You don't let Peg sing, we close down your chain.' I called Kopler and asked him to come to my suite. I also called the union men. Four of them arrived in dark coats and hats – tough.

Now remember, the entertainers who played the chain would all have been affected by the union's action. I told Kopler, 'If you are not satisfied after one week, I will work for nothing. But if you are satisfied, there will be no need for you to close all the rooms.'

Well, thank God, we were a big success. Sold out. I did many encores besides the seventeen songs. The children got to enjoy it all. Carlos flew in to take the bows. Kopler gave a big party for the union, the musicians and me. Great toasts were offered.

Afterwards Carlos Gastel asked, 'How did you do that?'
I said, 'I did not do it.'

Carlos said, 'I've got a lot of money bet on a football game. Would you, uh . . . pray for – '

'I don't pray for bets. If a football player had an injury, I'd pray for him. But not to win money.'

Carlos always thought of me as being on cloud nine, but I'm as practical as anyone you'll ever meet. I know what it takes to make money. The actions more than the words. If anyone makes fun of my beliefs, I just clam up. I just want to leave a residue of hope. I've always been a non-sectarian. I've always known it was between God and me.

As some of you may remember, the two biggest shows on television in the fifties were Ed Sullivan's *Toast of the Town* and the *Jackie Gleason Show*. David and I had hired Jackie as a warm-up act while touring, and I had no idea he was such a big star. But he said yes when we asked him.

One night Jackie and I went to dinner between shows, and later the manager came to me. 'You'd better talk to Gleason,' he said. 'He's very sick, I'm not sure he can go on.'

Well, he certainly hadn't looked sick to me at dinner . . . And then I realized he was only pretending to be sick as a way of getting through to me. At dinner, I remembered he'd offered to let me fly home in his airplane from Bridgeport, Connecticut, where we were appearing.

Later, I told Jackie, 'You'll be all right, I know you will.'

'OK,' he said. 'I'll go on, but you have to promise to stay in the wings.'

I agreed. And then, to my horror, he turned and played his entire performance to me in the wings, totally ignoring the audience. At the end he winked at me and said, 'How was that, Myrtle?'

After that he asked me if I would appear on his TV show for DuPont. When I did, I was standing backstage before we went on the air, shaking from fear. Art Carney came to the rescue, introduced himself to me, wearing a raccoon coat, and was . . . well, he was Art Carney. It did the trick and I was OK after that. In a way Art and I were like two school kids, Art always writing me funny notes. A lovely man.

New York – the Hampshire House. David and I were going to have a big party for the press in the Cottage Room, so I called Leonard Feather, hoping he would find me a good pianist to provide some incidental music. Who he came up with was one George Shearing, who had just come to the US from England and wasn't yet known.

During the party I was talking to some reporters when I heard this wonderful piano. I said, 'Excuse me,' and spent most of my time after that standing at the piano, just listening. That night was the beginning of my friendship with George Shearing. Later we would do an album together, needing to start from scratch, as it were, because George is blind and we couldn't use written music. We rendezvoused in Florida to set the keys and figure out the arrangements. We were up seventy-two hours straight.

When I'd start buckling from exhaustion, I'd call Ernest Holmes, who would say, 'Remember, you're not the one doing the work. It is not I, but the Father. He does the work.'

I would think about that, and it did help to refuel my strength and energy so that George and I could go back to work. I was involved, I realized, in a collaboration of more than two.

Meanwhile, though, David's drinking got worse. He talked about insects, I suggested he close the screen. And I even got an exterminator. But when the man came, David wouldn't allow him to do his work. What David did was throw a book at me. (He never liked me to read.)

I realized . . . I could no longer deny it . . . that I was getting stronger and he was getting weaker. I hurt bad, but my love for David could stand a lot.

When I came home from St Louis and points east and west, David went to Cuba for a vacation. Then one day, without warning, Daddy appeared at Denslow; smiling, eyes twinkling, looking a little thin. 'I just had to see you,' he said.

I was so glad to see him I started to cry. 'Here, let's go in and sit down. Would you like something to drink?' I tried to compose myself. 'How long can you stay? You will stay with us, won't you?'

'Yes, honey, I'll stay, for a little while anyway.'

I didn't know how long that would be, but it was so good to have him near. I had been working on an apartment over the garage – a practice room – as a surprise for David when he came back from Cuba, and it was perfect for a guest. I thought maybe Daddy would like the privacy of that room, but I wasn't sure when David would be coming home. Besides, I wanted Daddy close to me, so it was decided Nicki would sleep in her nurse's room and her grandfather would stay in her room.

Nicki's room was all white-dotted Swiss with pale pink piping, the furniture white trimmed with pastels. There was a canopy over the bed with yards and yards of organdy and more dotted Swiss, and the curtains were covered with miles of ruffles. It was about as feminine as a little girl's room could be – complete with a child-sized upholstered chair. Daddy, with his six-foot-two rangy frame, looked slightly out of place in the middle of all those ruffles – but he was happy, so happy to be there.

We got him settled, then we talked while we had coffee. We were both a bit reluctant, but he did finally tell me nothing had ever changed with Min. I hadn't thought it would. He said Milford, my brother, and Emily, his wife, were awfully good to him. I knew they would be, they were always so good to me. That was very important, because Daddy's life seemed so unfulfilled somehow. The fact he had finally had the nerve to make the trip out here – to defy Min and leave her behind – said a mountain of things to me.

As we talked I noticed his cough. He told me he had long since stopped smoking, so it wasn't that. I took him to Doctor Cavanaugh, who said after examining him, 'Peg, I wouldn't give you a plug nickel for his chances to survive over three months.' I felt myself sink into the chair. 'But, if you do exactly as I say, he could possibly last a year.' Well, that pathetic promise and my own fierce faith gave me something to hang on to, and I gave the doctor my word – I would obey him to the letter . . . and I would pray to God.

I began to repeat these lines to myself: 'Closer is He than breathing and nearer than hands or feet.' It is remarkable how close those lines can bring you to God, if you believe them. You might close your eyes and try them yourself.

Daddy and I didn't talk about his condition, we just referred to it as a respiratory problem but I stressed the importance of doing exactly as the doctor ordered so he could get better. He promised he would, but I'm not sure he believed me. Down deep I think he knew that constant cough was not a very good sign, but maybe he thought if he could stay with me, it would be worth the fight. Oh, how I wanted to keep him there.

We did whatever we could to make his stay happy. Daddy loved jokes, and I went about collecting them from any source I could. I called a lot of musicians – musicians are always good for a laugh. We also took him to see the family when he felt up to it, and I'm sure he was tired some of those times. He enjoyed the fact that I had a husband who loved me, a wonderful daughter, and a lovely home. He didn't know about David's problem; I didn't tell him. He was pleased with the lovely garden, the princess jacaranda trees, the fruit trees, my vegetable garden. He was glad to see my life had turned out so well.

And he was impressed with all the stars I'd met working with Bing and Durante. He asked me all kinds of questions about them. Nicki told him she liked Red Scallop and Jimmy Durandy. That made him laugh – and cough. He was so proud and absolutely astounded by my success.

The door to Nicki's room was always left open so I could hear him. One night I heard him crying. I went in – I didn't turn on the light. For so many years, I had lived in dread and fear of this time, and now here it was. Even when I was little, if Daddy had a little palpitation or anything, I would react in terror, thinking he was going to leave me, leave me with Min.

'Daddy? What's the matter? Can I get you anything?'

'No, no, honey, I'm – I'm just – realizing – I haven't been much of a father to you.' His crying made it hard for him to breathe.

'Oh, Daddy, don't cry. I love you. You must have done something to make me love you the way I do.'

It was a while before he calmed down. Finally, he fell asleep, and I went back to my room, wondering how long he had felt that way. He didn't know I had been listening. Thinking he was all alone, he brought up from the depths what he must have been holding inside for years.

He seemed better the next day. Then Min called and he said, 'Honey, I have to go back right away.'

There was no convincing him otherwise, though I pleaded. Knowing that if Min came out it would be unpleasant for us all, he was adamant about returning, so I arranged for my brother-in-law to take him home on the train.

We stalled around, wishing he didn't have to go, until we realized we would really have to hurry. We raced down to Union Station, and departure time was so close that we put Daddy in a wheelchair and went running down the platform to the train. Daddy, bless him, was laughing all the way. I know it wasn't easy for him, but it did make it easier for me. Maybe I learned about laughing from Daddy.

I would see him one more time.

There was always something going on at Denslow; just before David came home from Cuba and just after Daddy left, my brother Leonard and his wife Olie arrived without warning. I had to borrow the Stevens' pool house next door so that David's new studio wouldn't be taken up as guest quarters. I especially wanted to surprise David.

To top it all off, our second collie, Gay, had eleven puppies – a mixture of collie and Labrador retriever. I never did meet the Labrador, but David was a bit overcome when he returned from Cuba and saw all the dogs.

The next year, 1951, there was a gigantic statewide homecoming for me in North Dakota. People came from all over the state, including the governor and some *Look* photographers, and we all got caught in an unexpected blizzard. All communications were down. Telephone poles were snapped off for 100 miles around, leaving the live wires exposed. My brother Milford and I and Joe Cancelleri, who was working for us as a road manager at the time, drove through the dangerous area to see Daddy for what would be the last time. The highway department gave Milford special permission to drive in the area because he was a master electrician and could avoid the live wires.

It was a wonderful warm reception – I had not realized that the people in North Dakota cared so much about me. David was especially funny with the governor telling him he hoped he was a better governor than he was a singer. He was a good governor, by the way.

Back in California I tried to get David to join Alcoholics Anonymous by doing performances for them, but he knew what I was doing and wouldn't have any part of it. He would, however, go with me to entertain the members. Ironically, I later learned that some of the members thought I was the alcoholic, which rumour was strengthened by the role I was to play in the movie *Pete Kelly's Blues*.

The escalation of my career, the move to Denslow, the endless personal appearances, recording, promotional work, must have just been too much for David, and who should have understood that better than I? I used to garden as a hobby and found it very therapeutic – there's something about the soil that can be soothing – but David didn't have any hobbies to speak of. (He did try golf but the music publisher Mike Gould told me how Dave, when he continued to miss the ball, remarked dryly, 'Golf is harder than oboe.')

Finally, because David loved Nicki and didn't want her to see him drunk, he begged me for a divorce. In the end I agreed, broken-hearted.

It was easy to remain close to David for Nicki's sake. When I explained to Nicki that we loved her, and we loved each other, she seemed to understand. Unfortunately, though, she first heard about the divorce at school. I had wanted to tell her before, but David and Dr Stevens wouldn't let me. When it was time for the hearing, we were so friendly and obviously loved each other, the judge asked if it was a marriage or a divorce.

We did one final thing together with Bing Crosby and Gower Champion – the movie *Mr Music*. 'Let's Call It a Day' was recorded the night I gave David the divorce papers that I didn't want to give him. You can hear it in my voice. He took the strings off five guitars that night. Only once again did I get him to record with me.

David and I stayed very close all the rest of his life, even though he remarried for a short while. Somehow I feel we were never apart and he was a comfort to me on more than one occasion. We did have our difficult times when he drank too much, but what I really remember is love.

1951 brought another sadness. Daddy died in April. I was coming into Los Angeles on the plane. Something told me very clearly that my daddy was making the transition. Dear Daddy – I could see him everywhere. When we landed, Ed Kelly and David met me at the airport. That was unusual, so it reinforced my feeling that Daddy had gone. They were relieved that I already knew.

I reminded myself of what Daddy had told me when Joe and Mel took me back to see him for the last time. He and I had an opportunity to be alone and he asked me to read the 23rd Psalm. When I finished he said, 'I never understood that until now.' The room was still and then he continued, 'I don't want you to come back when I go. You go on and do what you're doing. Maybe folks won't understand, but *we* know, honey, and that's all that matters.' So I sent my sister and brother-in-law, Jack Martin, back to represent us, and that chapter of my life was gently closed.

5

The Movie Years

The 1950s were years of romance and suffering. I travelled all over the United States and part of Canada and made plans to go to Europe. I had to work to keep myself from grieving about David. Part of the time I toured with Billy Eckstine, Mike Bryant and Sid Hurwitz, starting at the Chase Hotel in St Louis and ending up in Vancouver, British Columbia.

Flying up to Vancouver, we had the experience of knowing that prayers are answered. We hit some rough weather. It was scary. The stewardess was so nervous when she couldn't get the door open to the pilot's cabin, she took a coat hanger and began to beat on the door. The crew, busy trying to keep the plane from being jostled out of the sky, couldn't stop to answer her frantic banging. It made the passengers afraid because it felt like something was terribly wrong and we were surely going down . . .

It reminded me of the story about Lifesaver candies, which they used to hand out during bumpy flights. On one trip it was *really* turbulent. The stewardess went around as best she could saying, 'Lifesaver? Lifesaver?' One of the white-knuckled passengers replied in a tremulous voice, 'Will that help?' After that the order came down to omit the term 'Lifesaver' and say 'Mint? Would you care for a mint?'

We were playing in a place called the Palomar Supper Club in Vancouver. My dressing room had no door, so the musicians used to take turns standing guard. The clientele was mostly lumberjacks, all heavy drinkers. It was a 'bottle club', that is, no liquor was served. You brought a bottle and were served ice and glasses. Having several bottles staring at you, I suppose there was a lot of 'bottoms up'. You also had to drink the entire bottle. After an hour or two, the fairly quiet gentlemen who came in were loud and boisterous. It was usually at that point that they would decide they were going to visit that blonde singer and see if maybe she wanted to dance.

Well, the fellows would guard me as best they could, and no one ever kidnapped me, but one night it all broke loose. There had been a radio contest before the show and the winner, Shirley Someone, was seated ringside – that was the prize. A nice, quiet girl, who had never been to a nightclub. The place was jammed, the audience was very drunk and I was quietly singing 'I Only Have Eyes for You' when suddenly one man cracked another over the head with a bottle.

'Are the stars out tonight? I don't know – . . .CRA–A–CK – if it's cloudy . . .' The fight was on. I called to my secretary Donna, who was standing in the wings, 'Where's Shirley? . . . or bright . . . Find Shirley! . . . 'Cause I only have eyes . . . Donna, find Shirley . . . for you, dear.'

The audience from the stage-centre all the way stage-right were trying to ignore what was going on at stage-left. That, of course, was impossible. They had already called the police. The paddy wagon arrived and they proceeded to pack half the audience, screaming and yelling, into the wagons. I continued to sing, while Donna raced out and grabbed Shirley.

Another memory of Vancouver is buying a dozen parakeets there and trying to smuggle them across the border in a hat box. (Someone told me it was illegal after I had purchased them and I didn't know what to do.) Joe Cancelleri, my road manager, had charge of feeding them apples and seed. I carried the noisy box under my mink coat. People stared and I nearly fainted when the stewardess said, 'May I take care of your birds for you, Miss Lee?' Not illegal at all . . .

Dear, patient Joe. He was always helping me out of some mess or other.

This was a time when I should have been home with Nicki more, but some of David's business activities had been extremely hard on our finances. For instance, we had purchased some choice land in the Doheny Hills from Ronald Reagan and Jane Wyman. It was three acres with a view of forever. The streets nearby had been named after birds, so we named ours Oriele Way and planned to build a home there. After maintaining the taxes for ten years, David sold it at a loss. In the late fifties, I learned from Sy Devore that a friend of his had made a killing on some real estate in the Doheny Hills – three million dollars profit. Sy didn't know we had owned that land.

The 1950s were a very creative time for me. George Pal of Puppetown fame hired me to do *Jack and the Beanstalk* and *Jasper's in a Jam*, among others. I was the voice of a harp in one film. After that George asked me to write some songs for *Tom Thumb*.

It was a thrill, of course, to see and hear Russ Tamblyn sing and dance to my newly created songs: 'Tom Thumb's Tune', 'Are You A Dream', 'One for You and One for Me', 'Sleep in Peace and Wake in Joy'. The orchestra played 'Tom Thumb's Tune' as a waltz, a march, a foxtrot and Russ danced it. I believe it had one of the longest playing-times for any single piece in a movie.

I recorded 'Johnny Guitar' . . . what an experience to have your own song be the title song of a film! Vincent Gomez played the guitar, Victor Young conducted.

Spanish music really interested me in those days. Laurindo Almeida and I wrote 'The Gypsy with the Fire and His Shoe', and Dan Daily tried to do a flamenco dance on the recording but it didn't quite work. Sammy Davis Jr came in and saved the day!

Las Vegas was roaring. I played the Sands for Jack Entratter, while Kay Starr was wowing them at the Flamingo with her 'Wheel of Fortune', Jane Morgan was 'Fascination' itself at the Desert Inn, the Ames Brothers were at the Sahara, Danny Thomas was playing, Don Ameche was starring in *Silk Stockings*.

The Copacabana . . . I played it many, many times. It was a spectacular place and part of the reason for that was the way Jules Podell, the boss man, ran his business.

Jules used to say in his gruff voice, 'The mirrors are always clean at the Copa.' In fact, the whole club and the kitchen were always clean. I can't say that for the dressing room in the Hotel Fourteen next door, but the Copa itself was kept in top-drawer condition. All of the men, maître d's, captains and all, wore immaculate tuxedos, and their shoes were shiny. The world-famous Copa girls were known less for their dancing than for their beauty. They would walk with their hands up and fingers extended as though they were drying fresh nail polish. Doug, the choreographer, used to teach them to walk in this manner. Three times an evening they dried their nail polish as they walked around the floorshow.

Jules was relatively short and strongly built. His neck was short; in fact, he seemed almost all of one piece, one solid muscle. He drank a lot, but he always knew exactly what he was doing. If Jules wanted attention, he would knock his big ring on the table and everyone would come running.

Tough? They don't come any tougher, as Mel Powell remembers: 'Once when Peggy was playing the Copa, she was having a big birthday party after the show for Jules Podell. It was a pretty elite mob, including Tony Bennett and Sammy Davis. They were all at a long table with Peg and friends of Martha and mine, including Nick, the Africanologist, and his wife. It was the early morning hours and the joint was officially closed. We were having drinks, food, a lot of laughs and birthday greetings, and a band was playing off in an anteroom. Nick, the Africanologist, was absolutely bagged, and when he heard the band, he wanted to go into the anteroom. Nick, a big guy, knew his way around. Suddenly he was a little assertive, there was a commotion, and he came stomping back. Out of the woodwork stormed Jules' boys. This was a tough joint. It was like a George Raft movie, with all the boys in tuxedos. They encircled Nick. Nick was about to be undone when Peg spotted him.

'She got into that circle and identified him as a friend of hers, faster, more sober, more serious than anyone had ever seen. Probably saved the guy from a bad beating. After all, they were protecting Peg, but she said to back off. For Nick, the protocol against letting yourself be shoved was tough to overcome.

'Peg had called Jules, and when he came into the centre of the guys, she said, "The man doesn't know what he's doing, he's just drunk."

'Peg was the one. I didn't see anyone else pay any attention. When action needs to be taken, that dame is going to take it.'

Jules was very protective, if he liked you, and he also did good things in secret, which are not well known. One day he called me and asked, 'Will you do me a favour, Peg?'

'Of course, Julie, what is it?'

'I want you to sing for some nuns.' Here was a man who only took one day off a year, Yom Kippur, and he spent the entire day in temple. Now he was asking me about some young novitiates in a convent! He said, 'I know the young nuns would like to hear you sing. "You'll Never Walk Alone" is one of their favourites.'

'All right, Julie, what time?'

'I will send a car for you at six o'clock. Then I can bring you back in time for the show.'

I was curious, to say the least. The limo arrived, I was taken to the convent, and the beautiful novitiates had nothing but good things to say about Jules Podell and how he supported the convent almost single-handedly. When I came back, he said in his gruff voice, 'Anything you ever want me to do, Peg, *anything*, you just ask me.'

You can never tell about tough guys.

I was doing a lot of writing in those days and a lot of recording. It seems to me that everything I really had to fight for turned out to be successful. 'Lover' was both exciting and difficult. Richard Rodgers was usually very strict about how his songs were interpreted. In fact, when we received his scores at Capitol, he would send instructions on how they were to be performed. All of us respected him so highly that we were happy to follow his orders. When I came to record 'Lover' a little bit later, I must have forgotten that. My idea for the song came from a French movie I'd seen where Jean Gabin played a very attractive man who had joined the French Foreign Legion because his girlfriend had treated him badly. As his regiment was riding out into the desert he waved a banner to change the gait of the horses. It struck me as I was watching that it could be a change of musical key. Raising the key would have the effect of seeming to go faster. Then the rest of the idea came: the gait of the horses resembled Latin rhythms, and if you start combining them – two and four, three-four, six-eight – it gets to be like the whole regiment is running off together at top speed. Then I thought, all I need is a song that goes with that rhythm, and, because of the star's love for the girl, I thought of 'Lover'.

I met with the rhythm section and said, 'Will you play this and will you play that and let me sing "Lover" about this tempo?' We started having a marvellous time. The bongos would be playing straight eights. The congas would be playing six-eight and other Latin rhythms, and the drums played a straight fast four, etc. We tried this in clubs and concerts, and people went wild over it.

I remember Hal March came into my dressing room one night and said, 'I just ate my shoe!' Chino Pozo got down on the floor and pushed the bongos the whole length of the dance floor with his nose! I got letters of appreciation from people like Pete Rugolo and other arrangers. It was something different that opened up a whole new world of ideas in music.

When I asked Capitol if I could record 'Lover', they said no because Les Paul and Mary Ford had a gigantic hit with their version, and they didn't want to create competition. I said, 'This is different,' but I could see their point.

I was at the Copa at that time, and one night Sonny Burke came in with Milt Gabler of Decca Records. When they heard me sing 'Lover', they got excited and said, 'We *must* have this.' 'Would you record it?' I asked. 'Of course,' they said. So I left Capitol for five years and went with Decca. 'Lover' was our first recording. They got the unforgettable Gordon Jenkins to do the orchestration, and we recorded it at Liederkranz Hall in New York. They had hired an enormous orchestra, with over thirty musicians, including eight percussionists, and back-up singers. I was so impressed and so thrilled when they started to play *my* arrangement. I thought I had died and gone to heaven. There was just one problem. They couldn't pick me up on the vocal. It was impossible with eight percussionists, and the acoustics in Liederkranz Hall are, well, a bit 'live'.

We spent the entire session doing 'Lover', not even starting the other pieces for the day. By the end I was in tears and said something melodramatic like, 'Well, it's just another dream gone wrong.' I went home to bed, and in the night I had a call from Morty Palitz, who said, 'Peg, I've been working with Charlie here, the chief sound engineer. We think we have the problem whipped, if you'll agree to go for another session.' Well, of course, I jumped at it, although it meant our recording costs doubled. I couldn't wait for morning to come.

They had built a sound booth (isolation booth). Maybe Morty Palitz and Charlie had a 'first' there – I had never heard of it before, and I don't think they had either, otherwise they would have set up the first session that way. I was a pretty happy lady when I went home that day, and so was everyone else – they were throwing their hats in the air!

When Sonny Burke heard it on the radio he said he pulled his car over to the side of the road and just sat there and listened to it. A lot of singers tried to do other songs that way, and many succeeded, but some didn't, because they didn't understand that the lyric had to fit the mood of the rhythm as well. 'Lover' was ideal for the technique because it didn't have too many lyrics – and they said the right thing – so you could break up the time while everything sails along under you. 'Lover' wasn't originally a fast tune, in fact Richard Rodgers referred to it in *Time* magazine, as 'my little waltz'. But he became so fascinated with my arrangement, he later told me, that when he gave lectures he would use 'Lover' as an example: 'If you don't change the interpretation of songs after a bit, they will die. They don't need to just stay in their original interpretation all of the time.'

'Lover' became the criterion for every drummer that worked for me: if they could play that fast, in four, not two, then they could have the job.

The producers Dwight Hemion and Gary Smith had the marvellous idea of asking me, Lena Horne and Vic Damone to do a television special as a tribute to Richard Rodgers. After the performance Richard Rodgers wired me to say that he'd never enjoyed hearing his music performed more than he had on that occasion – quite an honour. To top that, he then gave me *carte blanche* to do whatever I liked with his songs: 'You interpret my songs any way you like – I trust your taste.'

'Lover' gave Dave Cavanaugh, my record producer and beloved friend, the idea to do those Broadway albums *Latin à la Lee* and *Olé à la Lee*. *Latin* was a Grammy winner in 1960. The cover designs were my idea. I talked my gentleman friend of the moment into posing as the matador, in the 'suit of lights' for both albums. He didn't like that too much, and we broke up before *Latin* was nominated for a Grammy.

When Victor Young asked me to write some lyrics for him, you can't imagine how thrilled I was. He was like God to musicians. He was small in stature, but a giant none the less. His dark hair was greying a little by the time I met him in the early fifties (I guessed he was in his early fifties, too). When he talked to you he would make little karate chops with his hand, as if he were measuring off bars of music. I suppose the whole world was music to him. 'The bass line is the road bed, Peg,' he used to say. We had a mild hit with 'Where Can I Go Without You?'

He'd make speeches to my musicians: Jimmy Rowles, Larry Bunker, Joe Mondragon, Marty Paitch – all great jazz musicians. 'You listen to Peg, she knows what she's doing.' Victor was always helping some musician or other. He gave Marty Paitch his first opportunity to write for the symphony orchestra at that time. Jimmy Rowles and Marty Paitch did a lot of arranging for me – Jimmy, he's a champ!

If you came in with a Victor Young arrangement, everyone was impressed. Every now and then he'd drop an arrangement on my lap like a gift. 'Love Letters', for example, had five guitars on the recording, and he would sometimes come in and conduct.

I wrote a poem called 'New York City Ghost', which is about nine minutes long. Victor scored it for the Los Angeles Philharmonic and he also asked me to recite it in the Hollywood Bowl, which holds about 18,000 people. I said, 'Oh, no, I couldn't do that,' but he replied, 'If I thought enough of this poem to score it for the orchestra, you should think enough of it to do it.' Quaking in my shoes, with a temperature of 102, I did it. I was amazed at the tremendous reception it got. After the performance, I received an emergency call that my brother Clair had been in an accident and had gone through the windshield. I was driven to the hospital and sat with him all night. Thank God, he came through it.

I was confined to bed after that. To cheer me up Victor brought me a black lace nightie, and two themes from Schumann and Haydn – for me to write Christmas lyrics to. He handed them to me and said, like a tough little kid, 'Here – get better.' The songs became part of my album *Christmas Carousel* and later *Happy Holidays*. Billy May did all of the wonderful arrangements, as only Billy can do.

I was writing with Victor at the time he died, on 11 November 1956. He had just done *Around the World in Eighty Days*, right after *The Ten Commandments*. He was so pressured. He hadn't won any awards but had a whole bathroom full of Oscar nominations (that's where he kept them). In 1957 he was awarded a posthumous Oscar for Best Score for Dramatic or Comedy Picture for *Around the World in Eighty Days*.

When I first saw that face, I knew it meant trouble, but I also knew there was no choice. I guess I've never felt quite the same about anyone – except David. He said, 'Hello, I've been looking for you.' And for some reason I answered, 'Where have you been?' I don't normally say things like that to perfect strangers.

This was in Las Vegas, when I was still married to David, still very much in love with him. This Air Force pilot, a member of a famous squadron, had just come back from duty in Europe. Before that he had been a movie star.

The gambling tables were jingling and the chips were falling where they may. 'I just caught your show,' he said, 'and I've got to tell you something. We had your V-discs overseas, and I thought you were black. Can you imagine what a surprise it was to see this blonde Scandinavian walk out when they announced you?'

I could see by his look that we both had a problem. Even though David and I were having big trouble with his drinking, there was no room for cheating in my book. He walked away, and I didn't think I would ever see him again. But about a year later, when I was really on my own, he came to see me at the Copa in New York City.

After the show he asked to take me home. If it hadn't been snowing, we would probably have been riding in a hansom cab or something that lovers in New York do, but it was snowing, and we didn't want to miss the beauty of the snowflakes settling on our faces. We walked all the way home, and we weren't even aware of the cold.

He took me to the lobby and, wisely, said goodnight to me there. The emotion between us was so strong it held us in that wonderful spell that can't bear to be broken. Finally, we said goodnight . . .

In the morning I was still half-dreaming. He called me, and I knew it was all true and would remain that way. It did, through months of pure joy and tears and laughter . . . and then years of frozen memory. He wanted to be married. I wanted to be married. My divorce from David was final. Nicki, at the age of seven, fell in love with him too.

He and Nicki had the most charming arrangement. Every Tuesday was *their* night out, and I was not allowed to go. They went to places like the Plaza or the Tavern on the Green. They rode in hansom cabs and would go dining and dancing and come home laughing and singing. He would carry her piggy back up and down the stairs.

He took me to the races and baseball games. We went to the opening nights of *The King And I* and *South Pacific* and *My Fair Lady*. We dined at Danny's Hideaway almost every night, except when we went to the Drake and listened to Cy Walter. Night after night we would finish our evening with a few sets at the Embers and listen to Joey Bushkin or Erroll Garner or Red Norvo. We drove in the country and found little places to go, and we fed the ducks on the river at Westport.

We planned to be married in Greenwich, up in Connecticut. He bought me an antique wedding band – a hair ring in which he placed a lock of his hair and mine.

He was working on Broadway, and I'd meet him every night at the Henry Hudson Theatre. He had been separated for some time, and I had rationalized that it was all right. He went back to California to ask his wife for a divorce. I was so in love with him, nothing mattered.

But he didn't get the divorce. He offered to give up everything he had ever made, but his wife told him that wasn't enough. She must have loved him . . .

He came back to New York with his wife, we separated, and I went into shock. Finally I started dating again to try to pull my life together. One night we ran into each other at Danny's Hideaway. He couldn't bear to see me with another man. His wife saw his grief and left for California that night. Through a mutual friend he asked if I would take him back. Of course, I would. In my heart we had never been separated. Then his wife became ill, and he was reconciled with her . . .

Through the years he had several small romances, but every once in a while he would come to me and plead for us to find a way to be together. Each time I sent him back.

He became more and more of a star. While making his last movie, he called, and we planned to see each other again. After all those years. We made a date, and then we broke it. He called once more and said, 'I think I've hurt you enough, but you know I will always love you.'

A month ago he died.

One day in 1952 Sonny Burke called and said, 'Would you like to write a score with me for Walt Disney?' Sonny was the Artists and Repertoire man at Decca, where I was under contract.

Well, of course, a Disney credit was something to be devoutly grateful for, and I didn't even have to seek it. I didn't mind surprises like that at all!

Sonny and I went out to the studios to meet the great man. Charming? Yes, he was. The first thing he said when called 'Mr Disney' was, 'Walt, please. Everyone calls me by my first name.'

He introduced us to the entire staff – the artists, the animators, the sound engineers – and showed us all around with the enthusiasm of a young boy. Enthusiasm seems to be one of the keys to greatness, I've noticed.

Then he brought out the story boards, the preliminary drawings from which the animators would work. Walt began to tell the story of what was to be *Lady and the Tramp* as he moved along the board and asked Sonny and me to think of spots where songs would work.

Walt was encouraging about everything. I remember getting so involved in the songs that I wrote an extra eight bars to the lullaby 'La La Lu' that 'Darling' sings to the new baby. 'Lady' is at the bottom of the stairs – ah, but there weren't any stairs. Here's the magic of Walt Disney. He heard the demo I sang to inspire the artists and said, 'Well, this must be added to the footage where Lady is feeling very insecure about the new baby,' and so it was . . . 'What is a Baby?'

This might seem like a small thing to do, but imagine how long it took to paint each picture of Lady with the four paws moving slowly up the stairs and singing the lyrics with different expressions on her face. Those artists were incredible!

In the original story, 'Old Trusty', the bloodhound, was killed by the wagon. By this time every character was real to me and I started to cry.

Walt said, 'What's the matter, Peg?'

'That's too sad, Walt. *Please* let him live, please don't let him die.'

'You need the drama! If everything goes along too evenly, you don't have a story.'

'Yes, but it's just *too* sad.'

'Well, I'll see what we can do, but the *rat stays*.' Do you remember the rat? He really was a villain, and he played his role to the hilt.

One day Walt asked to speak to me privately. 'We have a delicate problem, and I wonder if you'd help us with the solution?'

'Yes, Walt, what can I do?'

'It isn't what you can do – it's really your permission I'd like.'

'My permission?'

'Yes, you know the little dog Mamie, from the dog and pony circus?'

'Yes.'

'Well, the first name of Mrs Eisenhower, our first lady, as you know, is Mamie, so I wondered if you'd mind if we named the little dog after you.'

Mind? I was thrilled to have him name that dog 'Peg'. The animators had me lip-sync 'He's a Tramp' and do a little undulating walk. So that's how I became a dog. I enjoyed being a dog so much

I decided to try being two cats – Walt chose me to be the Siamese cats and 'Darling' the mother. One of the things I enjoyed the most was being turned loose in the sound-effects department to find the sounds that fitted the Siamese cats. Bells, cymbals, chimes, the works. I practised singing one cat and then the other – a fifth away. Walt let me have all the freedom one could have.

Every person who worked on that film was touched by Mr Disney's genius. An Italian award given to *Lady and the Tramp* read: 'In this troubled world, a visible island of poetry.'

The picture was finished in 1955. Sonny and I worked for hire, which for me meant 250 dollars a day, or a total of 3,500 dollars over a period of three years. That's really not very much for originating four voices, especially considering the billions the film has made. Over the years *Lady and the Tramp* has been reissued again and again and in 1988 it was the top seller in video cassettes, outselling *Top Gun* and *Crocodile Dundee*.

I have been happily promoting *Lady and the Tramp* for those thirty-two years. In November 1987 Disney contacted me to do some more promotion work, only this time it had expanded to a satellite venture. We were driven out to Disneyland in Anaheim and got up at 3.00 a.m. to be made up and ready for camera. I was interviewed sitting in front of the big Disney castle and I believe I talked to eighteen or twenty-two cities all over the United States and Canada. Besides the satellite interviews, I did others in my living room in Bel Air, one after the other, all day long. For all this they offered me a small honorarium of 500 dollars!

One interview I did for CBS radio in San Francisco caused Disney some public embarrassment they deserved. I had just finished a long, detailed description of how I originated the duet with myself – singing the first part and then overdubbing myself to get the effect of the Siamese cats singing as Siamese twins: 'There are no finer cat than I am,' to rhyme with 'Siam'. The engineer put the needle down on the record and two strange voices came out singing, 'There are no finer cat than *we* are,' which of course does not rhyme with *Siam* or *I am*. I was shocked and said, 'That isn't even me. How dare they do this.' At this point, the show's host told the engineer to stop the record, and we briefly discussed the possibility that this was a bootleg record. It wasn't. It was number 1234, I believe, which is no longer released by Disney. I received a sort of apology from the product manager at Disney.

I sang a lot at Ciro's when it was *the* most elegant place you could go. It was also inhabited by the most eligible bachelors. Easily one of the most handsome was Greg Bautzer, who was highly thought of by every beautiful movie star around, including Lana Turner, Ava Gardner, Joan Crawford. This handsome lothario used to send me the most magnificent flowers, jewels, and other beautiful things. One was an ostrich made from a big black pearl with a ruby eye and a diamond tail. But the nicest thing he ever did was to like my poetry enough to have a private printing of a little book called *Softly, with Feeling.*

He often came to Ciro's. Herman Hover was the owner and it was frequented by a lot of Hollywood stars, including Merv Griffin and Judy Garland. George Schlatter worked for Herman, and we were always dreaming up some light-cue or other.

Whenever Greg and I went out to dinner – it seemed to me it was every time – just after we arrived at the restaurant, there would be a phone call from Howard Hughes. Greg would say, 'I'm sorry. I have to leave.' He would take me home and go off to meet Howard. After a while I guess I thought he was better off with Howard Hughes, so I changed the scenery for myself. Howard Hughes then gave Greg a brand new white Cadillac convertible, which he drove straight up on my lawn! I wonder if that's what I got for telling Howard Hughes I didn't like his Constellation when I was singing in Vegas? Howard Hughes and Jimmy Roosevelt flew in for dinner and to hear me sing. I was impressed – no one flew anywhere for dinner before the advent of the jet set. When they came to Vegas, Jimmy, trying to give me tips for conversation with Howard, whispered: 'You know, he likes airplanes.' I promptly said, 'I love flying. But there's only one plane I don't like – the Constellation.'

Later Jimmy told me Howard built the Constellation, but at the time I didn't understand when Howard gave me a grim look. That *mot* of mine ended our conversation, at least for that night. My problem with the Constellation had started one time when I was on a flight and looked out the window to see what appeared to be an engine on fire. The cowling was white hot. Burt Lancaster happened to be sitting next to me, on his way to Hollywood to make his first movie, *The Killers*.

'What's wrong with that motor?' Burt said.

'I've watched it go from red hot to white hot,' I said. 'It must be burning inside.'

Though we landed safely, the Constellation was grounded after that.

Howard Hughes stories are the stuff of legend. Once he crashed a plane into a house in Los Angeles and was taken to Hollywood Presbyterian Hospital. My thoracic specialist, Dr John Jones, who was also Humphrey Bogart's doctor, told me that the first thing Howard had asked for in the hospital was his hat. He had to have that hat. When he left the hospital after a few days, he had a truck come and load his hospital bed and take it home with him. He'd become attached.

Hughes would always send an emissary to make dates for him – in an old Chevrolet. He didn't like to be seen. When an emissary called on me, I said, 'I'm happily married and I don't play around.' Later, Howard hired David to do the film *Secret Fury* with Claudette Colbert. David, loving a play on names, called it *Secret Furrier*.

One night after I finished my performance in the Venetian Room at the Fairmont Hotel in San Francisco, I had a date with Hal March, who had come to visit me. We went to a little place in Chinatown, but found the place was closed. The man who owned it recognized us and said, 'Come in and have a drink. It's not against the law if I *give* you a drink.'

So, we went in and sat down. Hal was a very funny man, and he was regaling us with his jokes. It was so dark in there it made it all very mysterious. There was a retired army colonel behind the cappuccino machine, and at the far end of the bar I could see an Oriental friend, who turned out to be Paul Wing of Toy and Wing, a vaudeville act I had worked with years ago. We weren't doing anything but laughing when all of a sudden there was a banging on the door. The owner said, 'Get in the back, get in the back!' We ran to the back, tripping over a Harley-Davidson motorcycle and proceeded to hide behind it in a little alcove in the wall. It seemed a perfect place to hide. We crouched down, heard voices, and sure enough, the police came in, right back to where we were, playing a flashlight along the wall.

They could see our eyes. 'Come out of there,' they said. We didn't move. For no reason we felt as though we had done something wrong, broken the law. Fugitives. Well, we had to come out, nearly knocking over the Harley-Davidson, and explain what we weren't doing there. After the police were satisfied that we hadn't bought a drink, they left; we were left shaking.

'You'd make a lousy burglar, Peggy,' the owner said. I asked why. 'Because you left your beaded bag on the bar.'

Another time I was singing at Ciro's, Mike Curtiz came in to catch the show . . . perhaps Danny Thomas sent him in, I don't know. At any rate, he asked me if I wanted to do a film. Naturally, I was elated, but I think I suspected it was just another Hollywood conversation. Not so. The next morning I read it in a column, and the next thing I knew, Mike Curtiz was taking me out to meet Jack Warner to talk about making *The Jazz Singer*.

They introduced Howard Shoup, the designer, and he began to pour out designs for the character of 'Judy'. I was fascinated by the lovely clothes, so beautifully made and fitting so perfectly.

I knew Danny Thomas slightly from seeing him perform or running into him at benefits, but now we were thrown together going over the script, the music and the millions of details that go into making a movie. Danny was a dream, and we established a friendship that will last for ever. We laughed and sang and had a marvellous time while we worked like there was no tomorrow. Danny remembers it with affection. 'I have known Peggy for a long, long time. I was a fan and still am. We made the best version of *The Jazz Singer* . . . the first one was Mr Jolson, which was very badly filmed, the first Vitagraph. Edward Franz played my father; Mildred Dunnock the mother; very *nice* Philadelphia people. And we had this beautiful synagogue. At the end of the picture, they wanted to make Peggy Jewish; and they did, too. It was in the scene where she had come to visit for Passover. As her feet were leaving the screen, you heard her say, "I haven't been to a seder since I was a little girl." I fought with Steve Tillingham . . . "Leave it alone, for God's sake. What's the matter with this guy being in love with a non-Jewish girl?"

'You knew Peg hadn't been an "actress actress" any more than I was an "actor actor". We're both entertainers. Well, my God, she's Peggy Lee. Her name sums it up: she's an American treasure.

'That's why I get steamed up when I see a rerun of *The Jazz Singer* on television, and they edit out her song "Lover" in that nightclub. They also edited out all my songs. I didn't mind that, but not to have *her*? They're crazy. They have so many commercials, they edit out anything they want to get in many, many minutes of commercials. Cutting anything that Peggy Lee sings is to me a mortal sin. Oh God, she is so good.

'Her stage presence is so sweet, there's no cockiness about Peggy Lee. There's a big difference between ego and assurance. Peggy has no ego, but she certainly has assurance. I mean, she takes the stage, and I think that's the hallmark of any good entertainer. Not to be nervous. Not to be scared of the people. To take over . . . She conducts an audience the way a conductor conducts a symphony. She gets anything she wants from them. If she wants them to cry, they'll cry, and they'll laugh with her. She is quite a lady. Nature has dealt her a lot of blows, but she's gotten up and won every time.

'I had a great time with her on *The Jazz Singer*. We'd go off in the corner and rehearse our lines together. One time she got in an argument with Michael Curtiz – a great director, but, being a Hungarian immigrant, he wasn't too great with the English language. In the early shootings he wasn't too happy with her *or* me, we weren't giving him exactly the emotions he wanted. Peggy said to him, "I don't know, Michael. The way you talk and what you want . . . suddenly a door closes between us."

' "Now, Peggy," he said, "this time we are going to have a great scene, and we don't talk about no goddam doors." We all busted up laughing. She did too. But he got it out of her. He got it out of all of us. At the end of a scene, he'd say, "Excellent, we do it again." And he'd cry every time if you really moved him.

'I got requests for more pictures with her, but she was busy, and I was into *Make Room For Daddy* eleven straight years. But I adored working with her. Love her now.'

Somewhere in the whirl of my life I met actor Brad Dexter, probably at Ciro's and the Mocambo. Brad was playing movie heavies at this time. He was good-looking for a heavy, with electric blue eyes. What a big, sweet, lovable man he was. He was so good to me, and I was in such a muddle trying to do the proper thing. I was dating furiously; you might say my dance card was filled. I was grieving for David, I was also ill to the point of being hospitalized, and I hadn't forgotten the Broadway star.

I pored over Ernest Holmes' textbook, *Science of Mind*, and read everything else I could, trying to make some sense of it all.

I wanted a home and a father for Nicki, and Brad was good to her. He seemed to genuinely love her. I found myself loving his kindness. He liked to work in the garden with me; we liked going boating and dancing; we seemed to have a lot in common.

Brad's career was just beginning to build, and Ernest said, 'Are you going to get married?'

He caught me off guard and I said, 'Yes, I think so.'

'When is all this going to happen?'

Well, Brad got on the phone to me, and the first thing you know, we had set a date and asked Ernest to perform the ceremony.

Greg Bautzer had been running first, but I put cold water on that by laughing when he asked me to marry him. What a stupid fool I was! My low self-esteem quality came to the foreground again. However, we did remain friends.

For the big event we had a tent in the seven-eighths of an acre at Denslow and filled the entire garden with beautiful flowers. I can still see Ernest's dear smiling face. My metaphysics teacher Anne Wright was my matron of honour, and she brought all the aristocracy of the southern belles with her.

I was upstairs trying to get into the gown Howard Grier had designed for me and having all the jitters a bride could have. Penny Bozocos was doing special things to my hair, weaving in flowers and magic, when a new face appeared – one that would be with me for some forty years. Lillie Mae Hendrick. She came over to me, took one look at me, and suggested I take a little cognac for my 'pale little face'. I guess she became Mama Lillie Mae that evening. She helped me finish dressing and took me to the staircase. I had the bouquet clutched in my hand. There were about 400 people down there, including John Ireland and Dan Dailey, and the harps were playing like mad.

After the wedding Brad and I went across country on the Super Chief to New York for the première of *The Jazz Singer*. The publicity department at Warner Brothers must have told the press which train we were on – each time it stopped en route, people would push themselves through those metal doors and try to shove a camera in. Then I heard it – they called Brad 'Mister Lee'. I think that's when I knew it wasn't going to work. I felt so badly and couldn't stop thinking about it.

The première was exciting, to say the least. When the line 'I haven't been to a seder since I left home' came out of the screen, a wave of 'whatdid shesay, whatdidshesay?' went all over the Paramount Theatre.

Brad and I got along just great in many ways; it's hard to say why it had to fail. I came to the conclusion that I loved him, but I was not *in* love with him. Somehow I felt I was living a lie. I tried to tell him and asked him for a divorce. We had been married only nine months.

When he left Denslow, we were both crying. I hope he has found happiness.

After the divorce I went to live in New York; Tom Rockwell, the agent, let me use his duplex apartment on East 72nd while he and his wife Vivian were living in California. I had sold Denslow for a fraction of its real price because David, and then Nicki, echoing what her Daddy said, told me they didn't like the house. I should have realized that was just a pronouncement with more bourbon in it than common sense, but I was so shaken, I wanted to make them happy. That also was a twisted opinion with more emotional immaturity in it than common sense. A good friend told me they had found David among the packing crates one night with a guitar and a bottle, playing and crying. That did me in for a while. Nicki has since told me many times, 'Why did you listen to a child? Why did you *sell* it?'

In New York I was so lonesome for Nicki, and Alice too, for that matter. I'd been doing the Steve Allen early morning show, singing and playing straight girl for Steve, and drinking coffee with Lemuel the Llama. Steve was so nice, it helped my aching heart a lot. We also did 'Songs for Sale', and I had a programme for Rexall, but even all that work couldn't keep me from missing Nicki. Maybe I was saving the 'family farm', but I was running myself into the ground.

At Christmas I sent for Nicki and Alice to come to New York so we could spend the holidays together. Down to Grand Central Station I went, eagerly awaiting their arrival. Everyone got off the train, but no Nicki and Alice. I panicked. Finally, with the help of the good old railroad detectives, I managed to find them. Somehow, they had managed to make the wrong connection in Chicago. You can't imagine the relief to see my little girl coming up the platform – I had died a thousand deaths till then.

Alec Wilder, that superb composer and friend, pitched right into the Christmas spirit and came over, dragging a great big tree into the apartment as though he had just cut it down in the forest. We had heard of making snow for the tree but unfortunately had the wrong method. We whipped up boxes of Ivory Snow with the Mixmaster and as we covered the tree, its poor limbs bent lower and lower. Finally, though, we managed to finish it and turn on the lights!

It was really a lovely Christmas. Seeing Nicki again was worth staying up twenty-four hours a day, if necessary. I actually fell asleep in a chair in Hammacher Schlemmer, sitting straight up in the middle of the Christmas rush. They awakened me in time for closing. Alec joined us for Christmas eve and day. We did all the trimmings, Alice cooked a succulent goose, and Nicki loved the idea of *snow* for Christmas!

During the time I was working on *Lady and the Tramp*, Jack Webb called: 'I have a wonderful script. I don't know if you'll be interested in the role, because we're not going to shoot you in the best light. It's not glamorous, but if you like, I'll send the script over, and you call me as soon as you've read it.'

It arrived by messenger. I read it and immediately called Jack and said, 'I would pay to play this role,' which I almost did. It was worth every minute of it.

The part was Rose, in *Pete Kelly's Blues*, basically a nice girl trying to succeed as a singer, but not getting the right breaks, who becomes the girlfriend of a gangster and, because of their relationship, gets a pretty low opinion of herself. She starts to drink and becomes an alcoholic . . . Edmund O'Brien was very convincing in the role of the gangster, who's in the protection racket. He's Rose's man, and he goes to Pete Kelly to get her a job singing in his band. He forces her on to Pete, who was played by Jack Webb of *Dragnet* fame.

In the drunk scenes I had to sing off-key and out of tune. At one point O'Brien gets angry at Rose, beats her up and knocks her down the stairs. She suffers a head injury and goes crazy, and from then on thinks she's five years old and has a scar on her face. There is a rather famous scene from the movie when Pete Kelly goes to visit her in the asylum. She remembers nothing. She has a rag doll, and she sings a song called 'Sing a Rainbow'. A glimmer of something gets through to her and she says, 'Were we good friends?' Which is as close as she gets to reality.

When we shot the scene, I patterned it after a little girl I had known who was mentally ill, and when she'd talk, she'd stare blankly at me and say, 'Were we good friends?' I'd sing little songs to her and that one little good turn gave me the perfect way to characterize Rose.

Rose was my first important movie role, and I learned everyone's lines, which amused Jack Webb. Jack was also directing, and he said to me, 'I watched you sing and want you to do what comes naturally to you.' As we filmed, not a word of Richard Breen's script was changed. Jack Webb shot long master scenes as though we were doing legitimate theatre. The only problem was the noise on the Warner Brothers lot. We were in the path of the planes going over. Jack arranged to move us all over to the Disney Studio and use their sound stage. That made it possible for us to do Rose's big insane scene in two takes, and they used the *first* one, didn't cut it. This is a much more satisfying way to shoot a scene than the usual Hollywood method of letting an actor get out a word or two and then hearing the director say, 'Cut.' It let me really get into the emotional content of the scene.

Since *Pete Kelly's Blues* was shot for the wide screen, when it's shown on television today, you miss a lot. In the insane scene, for instance, neither Jack nor I are even on the screen. You can just make out somebody's nose. But at least the dialogue is still there, and the viewer has a sense of being there right in the scene.

They were wonderful actors in the film – Lee Marvin, Martin Milner, Edmund O'Brien and Janet Leigh. Little known is that Jayne Mansfield is the cigarette girl in the movie. She had red hair then, and she was beautiful.

Arthur Hamilton wrote the songs that Rose sings. I loved the new songs 'He Needs Me' and 'Sing a Rainbow', and I also sang standards like 'Somebody Loves Me'. It was difficult to put those words in sync after having purposefully sung them out of tune and time as Rose did in her drunken, confused state. Ella Fitzgerald was magnificent singing 'Hard Hearted Hannah' and the theme for the picture, lyrics by Sammy Cahn, 'Pete Kelly's Blues'.

I finished my part in the picture the day we did the insane scene at the Disney Studios. Richard Green must have done a lot of research on the character of Rose; she seemed to be a composite of so many singers I've known along the way, and I hated to leave her there.

James Dean was making *East of Eden* during that time, and he used to come over and visit me in my trailer – or was he coming to visit Rose? He'd arrive like a friendly cat. We were two shy people in a little room being very comfortable with each other. Jimmy was forever speeding around in his car, and it worried me. He was to die in a crash in Paso Robles, California, before he completed his next film, *Giant*. Jimmy was an unusual, quiet, intense person, and he wanted to be friends. He was one of those people you could not forget. You could feel things simmering and sizzling inside him, and his silence was very loud.

The picture completed, I moved out of Rose's trailer and said my farewells. There was to be a cast party when the picture was finished and I wanted to be there. At the same time there was also a personal appearance scheduled for me at the Lilac Festival in Seattle, Washington. My manager Ed Kelly, my hairdresser Penny Bozocos and I drove up there together, Ed Kelly at the wheel. Penny and I fed him radishes and ice cubes and used a lot of Sea Breeze and witch hazel to keep him awake while he drove all night. The only way to stay awake was to keep talking and singing and laughing. I don't think you can go to sleep when you're laughing, can you?

Kelly kept looking at an old covered bridge way up ahead and saying, 'Biggest goddam truck I ever saw,' but that's how it looked from a distance. We finally drove through it, and he was so surprised. I think he expected to hear a crash. Dawn came, and we were still driving; the radio was playing the current hit 'Good Morning, Judge. Why Do You Look So Mean, Sir?' That revived us a little. Then, having passed miles of beautiful greenery and trees and grass and picnic tables, we decided to stop in a peach grove that had been freshly ploughed. We spread our linen tablecloth on clumps of dirt and had lunch.

We checked into the hotel in Seattle, had a rest, I showered and washed my hair. Now it was time for make-up. Just before the trip I'd had some kind of heart episode; no real damage, but I was supposed to be careful. The doctor had told Kelly to be gentle, no big shocks. (He held my arm when I walked so constantly I thought we were joined at the elbow.) There was a bomb scare in the hotel: a bomb was set to go off at 7.00 p.m., but Kelly tried to tell me 'carefully' at about a quarter to seven – he told me there was a 'little

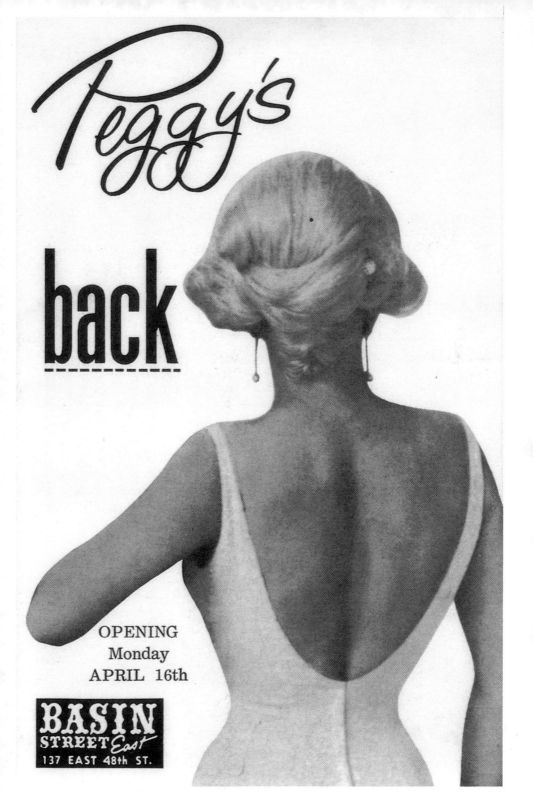

Peggy's back at Basin Street East.

Peggy Lee, Bing
Crosby, and Sammy
Cahn.
(Photo credit: ABC
Television Picture)

With Bob Hope.

Performing at Basin Street.
With a poster of J.F.K.

NEW YORK'S *Birthday Salute* TO THE PRESIDENT
SAT. MAY 19ᵀᴴ 1962 · MADISON SQ. GARDEN

Performing at the Florida Disc Jockey Convention in Miami.

A still from Pete Kelly's Blues, *1955.*

A costume for The Jazz Singer, *1953.*
(Photo credit: Warner Bros. Pictures, Inc.)

Sonny Burke and Peggy Lee while writing the score for Lady and the Tramp.

*Bing Crosby and Peggy Lee taking a break on
the set of* Mr Music.
(Photo credit: 'Mr Music')

Peggy Lee and record producer Quincy Jones.

Peggy Lee and Andy Williams.

With Tony Bennett.

*Going home to see Daddy
for the last time.*

Peggy and Ronald Reagan.

A dear friend, Paul McCartney (Photo credit: James Fortune)
At home in the Tower Grove Drive residence. (Photo credit: Hans Albers)

At the Queen Mum's Birthday Gala with James Cagney and the Queen Mum.

In front of the Sydney Opera House, one of the finest in the world.

With Edye Gorme.

With Ray Bolger. (Photo credit: James Fortune)

Singing 'Fever'. (Photo credit: Bob McKinley)

Today, with a friend.

fire' in the hotel. I kept saying, 'I can't smell any smoke. Where are the fire engines?'

He pointed out that the windows were closed. 'There *is* a fire, we *do* have to get out.'

'Are you kidding me?'

'No,' he said, and I could see he was serious. I was still putting on my make-up for the show, while down below the bullhorns were telling us to evacuate. Kelly made three trips to tell us to get out. He had already warned the musicians, and they were gone. Penny was busy getting the jewellery. She had set my hair with beer (at that time, beer was supposed to be the best thing to set your hair), and, because it was such a large stage, I had decided to use grease paint. Also, Dan Dailey had told me I never wore enough make-up, so I let the pendulum swing the other way. My suit had a large white ermine shawl collar, and I managed to get grease paint all over it. I also had a new heather mink that year, now covered with grease paint too.

Kelly said evenly, 'We have to get out. There – is – a – bomb – in – the – hotel.'

'Oh – OK, OK,' I said as I locked the door. Kelly, who was already running down the hall, shouted, 'Don't lock the door, it takes too much time.' I ran back and unlocked it. Kelly said, 'Oh, my God – I don't believe her! She's going back *in* again!' We now had about ten seconds left, according to the police.

All the news cameras were there, but the police kindly put me in their squad car. I was such a mess – a blob of make-up and beer – that probably no one would have recognized me, but they were saying something about Peggy Lee is here for the Lilac Festival. Kelly had our car brought out and we raced to the theatre, late for the performance.

We were so tired we were punchy. I dressed in some temporary shelter at the festival and the show went on. Straight afterwards I washed off all the grease paint and we went spinning down the road. Kelly was a great driver and he was determined to get back for the cast party, but as Quincy Jones and I used to say, 'Even a mink has to lie down sometime.' We had to stop and rest.

So we drove into a motel, went to bed for about two hours, got up and filled the car with gas and ice cubes and took off again for LA.

At first there was *no* traffic, but finally another car showed up and tailed us until we finally slowed down to let them pass. Do you know what we did – three grown-up people? We stuck our tongues out at them and Penny and I stuck our thumbs in our ears.

Have another radish, my dear.

We did make it back for the cast party and there was a lot of excitement about the film and a lot of talk about my character 'Rose'. It was, as Jack predicted, a highly successful role for me. I could hardly believe it when I won the Audience Award, the Laurel Award and the New York Film Critics' Award and was nominated by the Academy for Best Supporting Actress. Jack said I would not win the Academy Award because I wasn't signed to a studio, but being nominated by your peers meant the most.

On Oscar night Jack Lemmon and I were co-presenters. Some make-up person, with all the best intentions in the world, thickened and blackened my eyebrows, so I think Jack thought I was Groucho Marx. I thought so too.

I didn't expect to win, so I wasn't disappointed, and it's rather nice that after all these years, someone will say to me, 'I still think you should have won.'

After selling Denslow I was looking for a home again. The real estate person said, 'You'll love this house. It belongs to a writer and he's off in Europe someplace.' I learned there had been many, many tenants and each one had left at least one layer of wallpaper on the dining-room walls. 'It's all right if you want to decorate it your way. They all do,' the realtor said. When I saw the house, it seemed just right, tucked away in Coldwater Canyon, Beverly Hills, with lots of trees and shrubs and ivy – cosy, isolated. It had three bedrooms and a pool house.

Of course, no one told me it was haunted, and if they had, I wouldn't have believed them. Alice Larson, my housekeeper, wouldn't have either. She was too sensible. Maybe my sister, Della, or my brother-in-law Jack. Not me either.

My manager Ed Kelly and I were planning a big tour but first I wanted to redecorate. As soon as I pulled up the window shades I saw why they had been pulled down in the first place: it wasn't cosy, it was downright tacky. We began painting before we moved in, and it was someone's idea that everybody should paint a little: family and friends, lots of friends – a paint party. We ordered so much paint the manager of the department came over to see what we were doing and, don't you know, he joined too?

The dining-room wallpaper had to be steamed off to remove it. It was so thick it could have been used for soundproofing. Things would go along quite nicely until the cocktail hour and then whoever came over – doctors, lawyers, merchants, chiefs – would make a mess of something and it would have to be redone. We painted not only the inside but also the outside of the house. It was as busy as a beehive. The walls were wheezing with music and laughter.

The first night I slept in the house there were no ghosts – or else I slept through the floor show. I was too tired to be disturbed by anything. The first odd thing I noticed was my daughter Nicki dancing with the weeping willow tree when she came home from school, but that seemed normal enough for a young girl. Then Alice told me, giggling, that she saw the kitchen stool walk across the floor. Alice was a very practical woman but she always giggled a little when she got nervous – if she broke a vase, she would laugh as she told me. Soon everyone started mentioning they heard the empty coat hangers go dancing across the rods and two of us heard a little popping sound that would go through the house, but only at night. Then when Lillie Mae, who had been making lovely big hampers of food for the crew, came over with the last load, she let out a 'Oh, no, no, not *this* house!' She had worked there for a famous lady star who was living there with a very famous director. One night the star had been locked out in the nude when she went to get her dog who was barking. A tree fell on her.

Shortly after we moved in, the lights in the pool house started going on and off when no one was down there. 'That's Grandma,' Lillie Mae said. 'She passed away in that pool house and she's never settled down. Leave her alone!'

The lights by the front door started blowing out . . . we would hear footsteps and then my affectionate dogs would bare their teeth and growl, the hackles on their necks standing up. They *never* did anything like that. I've always had serene, sweet dogs. My sister Della walked across the living room, tripped on absolutely nothing and broke her leg. Off to the hospital she went. My brother-in-law became very ill. Off to the hospital *he* went. We all started calling the ghost 'Grandma' after the director's grandmother. I was never troubled, even though I heard and saw these things. The others said 'Grandma' liked me. I was flattered . . . until I got sick, really sick.

They called Dr Cavanaugh and he said I absolutely must cancel the tour. Kelly had to find out where we had sent Stella Castellucci's harp and Milt Rhinehart's trombone. I think we'd sent them to Boston. Kelly kept comparing it to *You can't take it with you*, what with the dogs wandering around and the piano being played in between some jazz records.

Dr Cavanaugh said, 'Thank God, you would have come home in a box.' Just before I left for a four-month rest in Palm Springs, I was sitting on the couch watching Alice and Jack Martin, my brother-in-law, bring some things up from the cellar. Jack said, 'Be careful, Alice, Grandma might be down there.' Alice laughed, but at that I saw the trap door, which had been leaning in the *opposite* direction, pick itself up and hit Alice on the head, knocking her downstairs. She stopped laughing.

We moved out and went to Palm Springs!

I came back to LA all tanned and rested and went back to work at Ciro's. Bob Calhoun knew I was looking for a home and he told me about a wonderful house on Kimridge Road. I couldn't wait, so we got a giant flashlight and went up to Kimridge that very night. Bought it by flashlight then and there.

It was even better than he said – brand new, with a view from every room. It was next door to George Putnam, whom I had known back in the Middle West. He had two adorable daughters who loved to talk to me through the fence. We added two new dogs to our menagerie. One night a little white baby Pekingese had fallen in the pool at the Sands. One of the fellows jumped in, tuxedo and all, to pull him out. I fell in love with that puppy while nursing him back to life and then had to buy him a mate so he wouldn't be lonely. I named them Little One and Little Two.

Life was great. This time I had the pleasure of putting in a pool and landscaping. My sister Marianne said my trees 'had wheels' the way I moved them around, but they thrived. Nicki and I were so happy with our new home, especially after 'Grandma's' house.

Friends used to say they always thought Kimridge Road was so romantic. Well, it was. It was cosy and lovely. It was a low-slung house on top of a hill with an Oriental look and a view of seven mountain ranges. The bedrooms for the ladies were soft and pale and pretty. Nicki's room had a white marble floor, mostly covered with white fur. Her bed was gold-leafed wrought iron surrounded by clouds of yellow chiffon. The canopy was caught back with gold-leaf antique carved wooden cherubs. The white marble continued down the hall to my boudoir, which opened on a private little garden with a trickling fountain. I've always loved the sound of water, the serenity it brings. I could meditate or take a sunbath there, maybe write a poem or a lyric or do a sketch to paint later.

Inside my bedroom the pale blue velvet king-size bed was up on a white carpeted platform. All across the back of the bed were white louvred shutters and on each side my dear friend Eddie Tirella had painted a wonderful *trompe l'oeil* – blue sky with wispy white clouds and a white railing which held two graceful white urns. At the end of the bed were yards of sheer white curtains that I could open or close by pushing a button by my bed. Magic! There were crystal chandeliers hanging from the ceiling, with mirrors that reflected the chandeliers for ever. Add a couple of pale green silk print Louis XIV chairs and a chaise longue and you have a very pretty bedroom.

Eddie Tirella – 'Eduardo' as I nicknamed him – made life a joy for me. Time after time the doorbell would ring and there would be an enormous basket of flowers with Eduardo hiding around the corner so he could watch my face when I saw his gift. 'Let's go to the nursery,' he'd call out, and I would jump into his Morgan car. We'd come back several hours later with the Morgan filled to overflowing with plants and flowers for the Japanese garden we were planting. It looked like a planter – the Morgan, that is.

We had a large fish pond built, about thirty feet long and a good four feet deep. We stocked it with perch, goldfish, carp, catfish and beside it planted a rock garden with ferns, ivy, moss and every kind of plant that would feel at home there. My favourite was a very old wistaria vine that was thick enough to weep over the pond.

One day I was dressed to the nines to go to a luncheon (which I seldom did) but I was ready for it with a beautiful Rex hat and a Jacques Fath suit. And, of course, in those days we always wore 'little white gloves'. (It became a code between Nicki and I. Whenever an occasion called for especially good manners, 'Nicki . . . little white gloves.' 'Yes, Mother . . .') I stopped to speak to Eduardo and noticed one fern jutting out of the rock garden. So, with all the faith in the world, I tiptoed around on the rocks . . . and slid into the pond among the lilies, the water hyacinths, and the mud. I managed to save the hat.

We had big mounds on two sides in which we planted Rangoon

lime trees, evergreens and plants that Eduardo had researched for a Japanese garden. We also built an authentic bridge over the pond to the pagoda on the other side. We painted it burnt orange and built a giant moon gate at the entrance. We hid a water pump among the plants so you could hear running water everywhere.

So many happy events would take place there over the years – a seventeen-piece brass choir playing 'The Lord's Prayer' on Easter Sunday, poetry readings, a classical guitar concert by Laurindo Almeida.

As a housewarming we gave a Japanese costume party. I didn't dare try the saki because of our guest list, which included our neighbours Charles and Prudence Elam, Alana Edan (a visiting Israeli star), Mrs Kuto, who played the koto (or was it Mrs Koto who played the kuto?) and Prince Edam (alias Eduardo). I was dressed as a geisha girl, in full Japanese make-up, and when Prince Edam grandly opened the moon gate for Jayne and Steve Allen, Steve said, 'May I please see our hostess?' looking straight past me. Duke Ellington very grandly escorted Mrs Kuto to the living room where she assembled herself elegantly on the carpet and played the most beautiful music. Duke was a wonderful guest. The warmth he spread around could get you through a cold winter.

I remember him bringing me the tape with the theme music from the movie *Anatomy of a Murder*. He just said, 'Here you are, Your Highness – write this.' (Duke had nicknamed me 'The Queen'.)

It seemed like a challenge to write a lyric about a murder, but for those of you who write lyrics . . . I just got lucky and found the poetic symbol: the fisherman. Jimmy Stewart played the detective who liked to go fishing and think about solving a case. The man who committed the crime, the one who will be caught, was the trout. I didn't have a symbol for Lee Remick, but her beauty was symbol enough. When I gave Duke Ellington the lyric he liked it all, and that was enough for me.

One very special occasion at Kimridge Road was a double wedding: my friend and bass player, Max Bennett, wished to be married to a lovely girl named Judy Stone, and his beautiful sister Mary, who was my secretary at the time, wished to be married to my drummer, Mel Zelnick. Well, what more romantic spot than the garden? It was to be a mixed marriage – Catholic, Protestant and Jewish – so

I asked my dear friend Dr George Bendall, an associate of Dr Ernest Holmes, to perform the non-sectarian ceremony.

I spent a lot of time planning the floral arrangements. I wouldn't think of letting anyone else get into that act! People saw this figure in white running around with a trowel and pruning shears, having a ball! I ran out of the garden just barely ahead of the first guests who came through the moon gate, frantically saying to myself, 'If I can't see them, maybe they can't see me!' Oh, and what a sight they saw! The curved bridge over the pond was all wrapped in white satin and white carnations. The pagoda was covered with lilacs, carnations, lilies-of-the-valley and baby roses. The back of the pagoda was a large fan of cymbidium orchids. The water was quietly gurgling, the harp was being played by lovely Stella Castellucci, and an occasional bird would fly over and pause on the wistaria weeping on the pond.

The brides were excitedly getting dressed in their silks and satins, and I was rushing into the shower before donning a special sky-blue organza with a matching garden hat.

Guests wandered through the house getting ready for the ceremony. The staff were seeing that plenty of champagne was being iced. There was a happy, busy hum everywhere. Little One and Little Two, our white Pekingese, were lolling on the Greek sheepskin carpet while guests tried to guess which was white Greek sheep and which was white Pekingese. (You could tell by the big black eyes.) The assembled friends were sending out rays of love to each other, and it was altogether a perfect ambiance for a wedding.

There had been no time for a rehearsal with Dr Bendall, so we had gone over the details verbally. Then the guests took their seats and Dr Bendall and the two grooms stood there in sartorial splendour waiting for their brides. Finally . . . the wedding march, and the radiant brides came out of the house and walked over the flower-covered bridge to take their places next to their new partners. Dr Bendall began the ceremony, reading some lovely lines from Kahlil Gibran's *The Prophet*. We were all mesmerized by the inner and outer beauty of the occasion but then there was a quiet rustle through the guests. I suddenly realized that Dr Bendall did not know the couples and, with the four rings and the double ceremony, he was marrying Max to his sister Mary! Mel and Judy just looked at each other wondering what was happening. I slipped in the side of the pagoda and whispered in Dr Bendall's ear, 'Stop the wedding, that's Max's sister!'

Well, of course, we had to laugh and begin again. He then pronounced them men and wives. I don't remember who caught the wedding bouquets but I know it wasn't *moi*.

Marlene Dietrich often came to hear me sing at Ciro's. I have always adored her, so it was a triple thrill when she wrote about me in her book. Then one day she called and asked me about a musician and I found she was truly friendly. She was looking for a replacement for her guitarist. In that low throaty voice with the delightful accent, she said, 'Hello, Pageeeee? Could you help me to find another guitarist? I have this fellow who plays only a plinka, a plinka, a plinka plink, and now he wants more money. What shall I do? Shall I just pay him zis money or perhaps you know someone else?'

She was, indeed, paying him well, and he was a fine guitarist but not quite so fine as to demand the salary he planned. I gave her a couple of names, and I don't know what came of it, but it strikes me that some people don't know how gigantic the demands made upon a performer, especially a woman, can be on the road. They add up, as the business manager says.

The fifties were a big time for clothes. Edward Sebesta was making magnificent clothes for me then, using all kinds of beading, wonderful fabrics, and feathers. He made me a giant cape out of *coq* feathers, which needed six hundred dozen feathers, and we were one hundred dozen short. The man who supplied the feathers was just fed up. It was a hot, humid day, and he was surrounded by feathers and orders for more – *coq* feathers, ostrich feathers, vulture feathers. He got very drunk and disappeared. And you know, I don't blame him. (Did you know they have to bleach and then dye vulture feathers. They're really beautiful. The thing is to get the vulture to sit still for all that.)

One day I was doing a style show for a charity event. It was all Don Loper clothes and Somper Furs. Van Johnson, one of the stars present, noticed I had an ermine coat to model. He said, 'Throw it on the floor, Peg, and drag it!' He gives good advice. (Last year, after my heart surgery, he sent me a wire: 'Sing out, Louise!')

Harry, our butler at Kimridge, had the highest recommendations
. . . I was told he had worked at Scotland Yard and had even been
a chauffeur at Buckingham Palace. Nicki and I were so impressed
we dressed up and stayed that way for the first week after he arrived.
Harry was most distinguished and preferred sit-down dinners – all
of the best silver, crystal and china were out for each meal.

One evening Art Carney was a guest and when Harry came around
with a full battery of silver, Artie dropped a serving spoon. In his
best Ed Norton manner he said, 'I beg your pardon.' Harry responded with his very quiet 'Carry on' (pronounced 'Ceddy on').
After Harry left the dining room, Artie said to me, 'Here's another
nice mess you got me into.'

The next evening Ernest Holmes came to dinner. Harry opened
the door to him and said in his very best British accent, 'Good
evening.' Down-to-earth Ernest stuck out his hand and said, 'Hi,
I'm Ernest.' My description of the brilliant and distinguished Dr
Holmes hadn't prepared Harry for that, but he quickly regained his
composure.

The other guests included Mr Arthur Carney, Jimmy Marino (a
protégé of Albert Einstein) and two geologists with bandaged heads
who had been in a plane crash. They had just returned from a
fascinating trip with Jimmy to a gold mine in Mexico, high in the
mountains with the Mayan Indians. Harry must have been stunned
by all of this, but he 'ceddied on' in his own impeccable way . . .
He later became the manager of a fine hotel.

Ernest Holmes loved to have Sunday night suppers, and would
do the cooking himself – I think his baked beans were the best ever.
One Sunday I met George Bendall for the first time, who was to
become a life-long friend. We were having turkey and George
accepted the honour of carving the bird. Carving was not his thing
– the turkey sailed all over the kitchen! We brushed it off, put it in
the broiler for a minute or two to sterilize it, and proceeded to have
dinner. We still laugh about it.

Hardly a day goes by now that I don't talk with George. I used
to do that with Ernest and when he left us, George took over; I
suspect Ernest told him to watch over me. Ernest and George were
like two guardian angels, and I remember once when I was very
troubled about Dewey Martin, Ernest said to me with great New
England candour, 'Now Peggy . . . you don't have to *marry* them
all.' Peggy heard but didn't always listen . . . I married Dewey,

and, later, the only explicit advice Ernest ever gave me – he usually said pray for guidance – was to divorce Dewey. Dr Barton said 'either get a divorce or a crash helmet'.

Jimmy Marino was not only close to Albert Einstein but to Robert Oppenheimer as well. I met this young man when I was singing at the Fairmont in San Francisco, he came right up and introduced himself as a fan, which was the beginning of a long and fascinating friendship. I was able to discuss my theory about colour and sound waves with this brilliant young scientist. It had begun when I had been chosen by Bing Crosby Enterprises because of the song I introduced, 'While We're Young', which I planned as a special feature with a screen full of colour patterns for a future performance. They were produced by my sounds hitting the chemically treated screen. I told Jimmy that I saw a connection between this and the colours I'd seen in my mind during an accident, when I was hit on the head. After my injury it occurred to me that those colour and sound waves might be used as a healing device. I still think so.

Jimmy was working on the H-bomb at Cal Tech, and he actually took my idea to Einstein, who, I was told, thought it had merit. He was even scheduled to come to dinner and talk about it, but that was just before his death. He did give me an autographed book, which I will always cherish.

Jimmy Marino and I had constant discussions about God (he claimed he didn't believe in God). He was short from having had polio, and he had a withered arm. Because he couldn't do physical things he would have liked to do, he poured everything into science. He often talked about the sorrow that Oppenheimer felt about the A-bomb.

Jimmy later invented a machine to refine uranium ore at the mine site, and was teaching people how to use it when he slipped and fell into the machine and cut off his good arm. They brought him to the Navy hospital in San Diego. I went to see him wondering what I could say to him. Before I could open my mouth, he held up his withered arm and showed me that he had learned to write with it. We never discussed what had made that miracle happen.

Jimmy came to live in my house to recuperate. He was there for nearly a year and I had a steady stream of scientists coming to my house.

Jimmy disappeared and all I have left are his books. He knew so much about the A- and H-bombs I really suspect he was either kidnapped by some other country or done in by someone who thought he knew too much.

How easy it is to 'love thy neighbour' if you have such nice neighbours as I had at Kimridge Road. There were the Putnams, who kept a cat I had adopted (part Bobcat, I think, I called him 'Rusticat') when we left there. And then there was Frank Sinatra . . . When I heard he was building a house near me, I was delighted – I was his friend for ever after the way he treated me at the Paramount Theatre.

There have been very few men in our business who have affected me so deeply I can't express myself, and Frank is one of them. Cary Grant is another, and Bing Crosby another. Yet we have been very close friends for many years in each case.

Frank invited me to his house so many times for dinners or parties or movies in his theatre. We also shared quiet talks, funny jokes and planned a whole album together. *The Man I Love* was first released on Frank's Essex label, a subsidiary of Capitol Records, and later was rereleased on Capitol. We were 'the folk who live on the hill' from the song of almost the same title.

The album was totally his concept. He brought me a long list of great songs from which to choose, and Bill Miller came over and set all the keys with me. Then Frank hired Nelson Riddle to write those lovely arrangements and Frank conducted them – a marvellously sensitive conductor, as one would expect. He designed and supervised the cover. He is a producer who thinks of everything – even putting menthol in my eyes so I'd have a misty look in the cover photograph.

Frank Sinatra has always been somewhere near – just touching the elbow, holding the hand . . .

6

Fever

In 1958 I wrote the special lyrics to 'Fever'; the first two verses were from Little Willie John's smash hit. I also did the arrangement. I remember the day I demonstrated it to Sammy Cahn and told him I wanted to use just bass, drums and finger snapping. (Jack Marshall, my conductor when it was recorded, won a Grammy for that arrangement.)

I had no idea my version would set off such a rash of fevers. My friend Pat Shelton, fashion editor for the Chicago *Sun-Times*, told me that when she goes to Paris for the big fashion shows they always play my recording of 'Fever' for the models on the runway. (She says that Sonia Rykiel also plays 'Why Don't You Do Right?', 'Don't Smoke In Bed' and others.) It gives me a thrill to think I'm there, in a small way, in the fashion world, but it shows how important it is to secure copyrights. I recently saw the printed sheet music of 'Fever' with my special lyrics but no credit for me as writer. That means I'm not credited with ASCAP nor with BMI. Watch your copyrights!

When my recording of 'Fever' came out in 1958, I had a recurring fever and had to go to bed for an extended time. I asked my doctor to give me a reason to tell the press. He said, 'Tell them you have mononucleosis; no one will know what that is.' Oh, yes? Well, I did just that, and someone looked it up and found it is also known as the 'kissing disease'. So a feature wire story went out saying, 'Peggy Lee has the "Kissing Disease", she has the "Fever" from too much kissing.'

Oh, the 'glamour' of show business. I'll never forget one tour we did of the South and Mid West. We were in New York City and while the crew were preparing to leave, Tom Rockwell sat listening intently to a news broadcast about 'Hurricane Hazel'. I wandered into the bedroom, where Lillie Mae and Stella Castellucci were busy packing the gowns and shoes and myriad things a woman needs on the road. 'What is Hurricane Hazel?' I asked.

'I don't know,' Stella said. 'I think they're naming hurricanes after women now.'

She was right and Hazel was a particularly wild lady. I went back in to talk with Tom and Kelly. 'Is there a hurricane coming?'

'No, there isn't, but there is one down where you're going.' Tom looked a tad worried. Now it was my turn to be concerned.

'Do you mean we're going to fly into a hurricane? Tom, I don't like the idea of that!'

'Well, maybe it will blow out to sea,' he said. That sounded good, but not good enough, so we changed our plane reservations and opted for a bus ride. We took off for Cape Charles with George Kirby, the Rugolo Orchestra, the Drifters, Ed Kelly and my group, and ran right into Hazel at Cape Charles. I've never heard a wind like that, she was wild all right!

We missed the first ferry boat, so four of us held hands and tried to walk a short distance to find something to eat. Anything less than four people would have taken off in the wind like paper dolls. Gene DiNovi was holding my hand, I recall, and was laughing and laughing, as was his style. We had to go back to the bus, which took off again. Mike, the driver, and Charlie Carpenter, the tour manager, thought that the weight of the bus would hold us down, but we learned that was not quite true. I remember seeing the neck muscles and tendons standing out on Mike's neck as he rode that bus like a bronco. Chino Pozo was hanging on the overhead racks and saying with his thick Cuban accent, 'I go anywhere with you, Peggy Mang!'

The bus was careening madly down the highway and at times the wind actually lifted it off the road. Big billboards flew through the air and the wind picked up a great huge tree and threw it across the road in front of us. Several of our fellows organized a way to push the door open. There was a hydraulic door on the bus but it was no match for the force of the wind. It really took some doing to move that tree. We were coming into Salisbury, Maryland, so we decided to stay and try to take shelter.

We found a motel. At first, believe it nor not, the owner didn't want to give us all shelter because some of us were white and some of us were black. He finally relented and we crowded in. Stella and Lillie Mae were understandably frightened. Well, we all were a bit unsettled, you might say. We learned that six people had been killed in Salisbury that day.

The motel was shaped like a U and from our cabin we could see the whole complex. Everyone came to our space, for some reason. We were wondering about the eerie stillness when suddenly the roof flapped like a petticoat and then flipped up and tore off. The whole roof came off *except* where we were!

Pete Rugolo and I were attempting to be scout leaders. I remembered seeing a sign advertising chicken just before we reached the motel. We all piled into the bus and rode back there. The owner was friendly, but in a state of shock. His electricity was out but the gas was still on, so Pete and I, chefs that we are, cooked everything we could find. The gas was still on. Mike parked the bus so the lights would shine inside, and we dined by bus-light. We hadn't found food since New York City, so we were hungry! Pete and I rattled those pots and pans and gave everyone a full plate. For dessert we had melted ice cream. By that time, the hurricane had blown out to sea and the relieved proprietor, when asked for the tab (there were seventeen of us), said, 'That'll be seventeen dollars.'

With very little sleep, we took off the next day for Raleigh, North Carolina. The rest of the tour was similar to the beginning. I think it was Raleigh where I lost my shoe. I was wearing a beautiful beaded lace dress by Don Loper and some fragile dainty sandals by Mr Sidney. The dainty little strap broke and, since I couldn't sing on one foot, I took the other shoe off. I called to Lillie Mae to bring my spare pair and she kept repeating, 'That's just the trouble, that's just the trouble!' as she threw things out of the trunks looking for the other pair of shoes.

Meanwhile, the audience, delighted, started bringing me *their* shoes, tossing them up on the stage. What sweet people, to give up their own shoes! After the finale it was hilarious: everyone began to try to find their own pair.

By the time we got to Des Moines our group was getting mighty sick of the bus, so we took a train for one night. When we arrived, the depot was deserted, except for a party of people loading a coffin on to the train. I saw the ambulance, ran up to the driver and asked him if he could take us to the auditorium. There weren't any cabs, so I had to think of something. He agreed and we loaded all our luggage and instruments into the ambulance. We made the ride a lot more fun for the driver than the previous passenger. We told him we were in a hurry, so he turned on the siren, but we were stopped by a police car. The officer stormed in the door saying,

'Who's sick in here?' Apparently, it was against the law to use the siren unless someone was sick. I admitted I was the culprit and he let us go with a stern warning.

A few more greasy spoons and we were on our way back to New York City and on home to California, where surgery awaited me. I had been told it was a probability before we left. However, it was only a small taste of what was to come in the future, which made me think of the hospital as 'the garage'.

After the operation Dr Garbak and Dr Stevens let me out a trifle early because it was Christmas. I celebrated it surrounded by men – Jimmy Marino, Dave Barbour, Dr Garbak, and Harry the butler, but when I tried to stand and walk to my bed, I fainted dead away! When I came out of it, I thought I smelled of vinegar and I was right. David and Jimmy Marino (both of Italian descent) had, in their nervous state, poured first vinegar and then olive oil on my head. They thought it was an old Italian remedy. I thought it was more like a salad.

So I spent a little time at home recuperating and gathering strength to go down to Palm Springs. It was so peaceful down there, I took my paints along and painted the beautiful mountains just outside the door.

When I came back home I was greeted by an unusual request from Countess Carpenetta: she wanted me to pose for a painting. She was a charming lady, and even though I was still tired from the surgery, I consented. I also found myself agreeing to her bringing an Indian gentleman along with her. They arrived with all her painting equipment. She introduced me to the young man, who was wearing a beautifully wrapped turban, and said, 'You won't have to sit absolutely still, perhaps once in a while, but I thought you might like to talk with my friend here, that is, if you wish, and I'll just paint away.'

As I gazed at the handsome young man with hypnotic eyes my thoughts flashed back to San Francisco in 1945. Molotov, the Soviet foreign minister, was one of the visitors there for the founding session of the United Nations. Police and security were everywhere. I was singing at the Fairmont Hotel and a group of fans were gathered in front of the hotel waiting for me to come out. As you can imagine, with all the heads of state and important people from all over the world, the police were shooing my little group of fans away saying, 'Molotov is gone, Molotov is not here.' They replied,

'Who is Molotov? We're waiting for Peggy Lee!' It was in the papers.

The San Francisco press had invited me to be a hostess at their reception for the UN delegates. To this day I remember it all with great pride. For being a hostess I was awarded the 'Black Cat', which meant that I could always speak 'off the record' and it would be honoured. (The honour is named as a black cat named 'Stormy', a survivor of the San Francisco earthquake. The story goes that he was found amid the ashes when the Press Club was destroyed by fire.)

During the meetings at the UN and the reception at the Press Club, anti-Americanism among India's representatives was apparent. I met Krishnamurti's aide and, as he extended his hand, he said, 'You are the only American thing we have in our home!' 'I hope that won't always be so,' I said ruefully. It set off a chain of events in my life that to this day amazes me.

Countess Carpenetta continued to paint that day, seemingly ignoring us, and as I looked back from my daydreaming at the young Indian, I had to ask him, 'Why does India have such angry feelings about America?'

'Because we don't get the complete picture of Americans,' he said. 'We see only violence and things we don't approve of. If an American finds a man down in a well, he would, from the political standpoint, dangle a rope a little way down while saying, "If you live our way, I will drop this rope down to you." All the while he is telling the man who is drowning, "You should not be down there." Well, along comes a Russian and he looks at the situation and gets a rope and without saying anything, he just drops the rope down. Now, which of these do you think the man down the well will choose?'

It planted a seed in my mind. Ralph Carmichael and I wrote a song called 'Meals for Millions' and we recorded it at Capitol Records, the proceeds going to Meals for Millions. We were working with Eddie Albert and a lot of good people, sending soybean flour – which tasted terrible, but not if you were starving in Southeast Asia – wherever we could to feed as many as we could.

At about the same time, in the late fifties, I met a handsome young doctor named Dr Verne Chaney, a thorastic surgeon who had given up his profitable practice to help people. I had not forgotten the conversation with the man from India, and when I heard of the things Dr Chaney was doing, I gladly accepted the title Madame Chairman for the Thomas Dooley Foundation, which preceded the Peace Corps by a few years. Ahead of his time, Thomas Dooley had seen the Vietnam problem, but he was dying of cancer, so Verne Chaney took over the whole project. We sent food, medicine and Disney films to Laos, Cambodia and Vietnam.

One proud day they christened a little hospital boat *The Peggy E. Lee* in Union Square in San Francisco. I believe I sprinkled Herb Caen with champagne when I hit the boat. (One other time, I really got him wet hitting a cable car. I really love Herb Caen.) The little hospital boat was sent over to the Mekong River and travelled up and down before and throughout the entire Vietnam War.

It was a wonderful feeling to be present in San Francisco again when the late Eugene Burdick (co-author of *The Ugly American*) presented the 'Splendid American' award to Henry Cabot Lodge for his work in Southeast Asia. But it was chilling to hear him speak about the terror of the Viet Cong planting severed heads on poles in front of the houses from which the heads came.

I could reflect back to the young man from India and realize that whatever we did was done without any strings but with great sincerity. So many wonderful things occurred as a result of that one conversation with a man I had never seen before, nor have I seen since . . .

Back in New York, one day Dr Verne Chaney and Thubton Norbu, the brother of the Dalai Lama, came to my suite. Thubton was carrying a little black and silver furry ball, which turned out to be one of the dearest things in my whole life: It was Sungyi La (meaning the Honourable Lioness), a Lhasa Apso. They explained that the Dalai Lama was aware of the work being done by Meals for Millions and the Thomas Dooley Foundation and they presented me with the Dalai Lama's book *My Land and My People*, a prayer scarf and an autographed photo, which I shall always cherish.

There is no charm like the charm of Cary Grant. I was playing at the Flamingo in Las Vegas. Cary Grant asked me to join him for supper after the show. As luck would have it, I wasn't feeling well, but told him I would surely be feeling better. He said, 'Why don't I just meet you in the lounge when you're ready? I have a feeling we're going to be very good friends.'

The second performance, I was weaker than ever, and to make

matters worse, I was wearing a fifty-pound beaded gown that Don Loper had created for me. (We called it 'The City of Glass'.) As I did my final step off stage with the gown propelling me along, it was apparent there was no way I would be able to see him that evening. I left a message that I was too ill and would he please call me? I didn't hear from him. Much later I learned the messenger had his own motive regarding me, and he didn't deliver the message. Mr Grant must have thought I was terribly rude.

Some time went by, and I was in New York singing at Basin Street East and living at the Waldorf when the phone rang one day, and that voice said, 'Hello, Peggy? Cary Grant.'

'Oh, *hello*!' My hands were shaking. I managed to pull myself together and enquire how was he. He was fine. I was fine. Would I get him in to Basin Street? Would I get him *in*? Yes! Any time, any time at all.

Well, he arrived, and naturally there was a to-do. He sat next to Ray Charles and Quincy Jones. He loved talking with musicians. By the way, did you know he played the piano? Yes, he played *my* piano – and he read music, too. He called the next day and asked if I had any influence on how to get *out* of Basin Street East. I said, 'Oh, yes, I imagine *you* would have trouble getting out.' 'Oh no, it wasn't that,' he said. 'There was just such a line of people waiting to get in for the next show.' He was impressed (I was flabbergasted), and we became friends.

After that, he used to call me and occasionally he would come over. He lived very near me. I would tell him a joke, he'd laugh and say, 'I can dine on that for several weeks,' or 'I need some new material.'

Once he was interviewed at some length by a writer for a magazine article. The writer finished the interview and left, then realized he had not asked all of the questions he had planned to ask, specifically Cary's age. So he sent a wire to Cary Grant's secretary: 'By the way, how old Cary Grant?' Cary's answer: 'Old Cary Grant just fine. How you?' He *was* ageless. It was so special to know him.

He asked me to write two songs for him to record for a charity, something for Christmas and something for the New Year. Dick Hazard and I wrote 'Here's to You', which Cary also recorded on Columbia Records, and I wrote the Christmas Lullaby with Cy Coleman. Cary recorded these two and one other called 'I Wound It Up', which I wrote alone. He wanted to develop it further so it was not released, and we never got back into the studio with it. He asked me to go to the studio and be with him when he recorded. He was uncomfortable about singing, not being a professional singer, and we would rehearse at my house.

Earlier Cary had asked me to write some songs for *Walk, Don't Run*, his last movie. I asked for Quincy Jones to do the score and I wrote the lyrics for 'Happy Feet', and 'Stay with Me', but they didn't get into the picture because I was once again hospitalized. Quincy's score was excellent and I was awfully glad for him.

When I was writing this book in 1986, Cary told a friend about how he called me backstage in Las Vegas all those years ago: 'A very sensible move on my part. I had always admired her talent. A most remarkable singer. She knows what every musician is doing. How many singers stand up in front of an orchestra and don't know what's going on? If a singer hasn't the awareness of what the musicians are playing, they can't possibly last as long . . . When you go to see Peggy, you know what you're going to see, and it's marvellous.'

You can imagine what that means to me – especially now. At the time I tried to explain to him, 'When you walk into the room, everything stops for me. After all these years, I don't address you by any name – never call you Cary.' And he said, 'Why Peggy! You know I've always loved you. Even my wife knows it!'

1959: Opening night at Basin Street East was electrifying. The red carpet was rolled out for the limousines. Kleig lights shot up through the New York skyscrapers. Stars and lights and flowers, everything shining. The orchestra was hand-picked. A lighting booth had been installed, and the lighting director had a myriad of light cues to play along with the music. The performance began and was lifted high by the enthusiasm and excitement of the audience. Standing ovations, bravos.

The reviews were spectacular, and the lines of people, four abreast, formed around the block. They continued to do so each time I played there. God bless New York! *Newsweek* credited me with 'single-handedly reviving the supper club business'. I sang and sang and sang. They loved it all, and so did I.

Phoebe Jacobs, who worked as an assistant to the owners and had been with Basin Street East since the beginning, remembers my first engagement: 'Miss Lee would require certain things: "Don't forget I need a sweet potato for that number." One of the proprietors, Mo, would say, "Does she want it candied or . . .." ' I also wanted a white rope, so they got me one rope from the *Queen Mary*. It looked superb on stage. The owners were wonderful, they looked like Laurel and Hardy or Frick and Frack. Mr Lewis loved to effect a tough-guy image, and Mr Watkins had exquisite taste and a manner very much like Rex Harrison's. They had opened Basin Street in October 1958, in the grand ballroom of a hotel at Forty-eighth and Lexington, able to accommodate 450 customers, including the bar and lounge.

'Basin Street started out to be a nightclub,' Phoebe says, 'but by the time Peggy got through with it, it was a concert hall . . . New York was Peg's.' Soon, people would call for reservations and say, 'How much will you take for a seat?' There was such a crowd on Saturday nights that Phoebe's son would make seventy-five dollars for keeping people in line and forming them into an orderly file when it was time for them to come into the lounge area. Sidney Roth ('Big Broadway Sid') was the maître d' at Basin Street East. The waiters lined up the tables bar-mitzvah-style to get as many customers in as they could, and soon there were 610 people at every performance. 'We had to hire only skinny waiters,' Phoebe says. 'It was a love affair between Peggy and the busboys, waiters and captains. They went home with bundles of money and would pool their money to buy her a gift or flowers. There's a waiter at Gallagher's who used to be a busboy at Basin Street East, and he was able to buy his house in Queens because of the tips he made when Peg was at Basin Street. Bob Kiernan, a lighting apprentice, learned so much from Peg about special gelatins, cues and colours that Frank Sinatra paid him handsomely to light for him at Radio City Music Hall.'

I could look out in the audience and see the likes of Judy Holliday, Quincy Jones, Ray Charles, Judy Garland, Tallulah Bankhead, Count Basie, Joan Crawford, Cary Grant, Ella Fitzgerald, Sophia Loren and Carlo Ponti, Marie and Jimmy Durante, Lena Horne and the faithful Marlene Dietrich. It was heady stuff.

This was a hectic time, because I was also doing a series of TV specials for Revlon with John Gielgud, Carol Channing, Alan King and Abe Burrows. I was doing two shows a night Monday through Thursday, three on Friday and Saturday. Dr Martin Stone, president of the American Medical Association, made reservations for every show every night. When New York had a big snowstorm, the mayor declared a state of emergency, and all moving vehicles were ordered off the streets. Mr Watkins, the proprietor, wanted to put a padlock on the door. Phoebe said, 'No. We have five hundred reservations, including Dr Stone. And all the people in the hotels around the club want to see Miss Lee.' The butcher and baker couldn't deliver, so there was no food. Phoebe went out and paid five dollars to school kids with sleds to go with her to grocery stores in the neighbourhood and buy all the chickens they could find. The chef, who was oriental, created haute cuisine. That night of the big storm, the club was filled and Dr Stone was at his usual table. He'd arrived at Basin Street East in a bobsled. TV crews showed up from every network. They couldn't believe all these people would go to a nightclub on a night like that.

Edgar Bronfman, chairman of the board of Seagram's Industries, frequently came to see me. Active in cancer fundraising, he asked me if I would chair a gala at 500 dollars a plate. Basin Street rented china, sterling, and crystal for the fundraiser. We had programmes and menus with all the dishes named after my songs. The proceeds went to the Runyon Cancer Fund, Meals for Millions and Girl's Town.

When I said I wanted to live at the Waldorf, Basin Street made enquiries for me. Henry Kaiser, who owned an apartment there, said he would love to have me live in his apartment while I was in town. Nicki, my hairdresser and I moved into real luxury – four bedrooms, four bathrooms, and a dining room the full length of the suite. Adlai Stevenson was my neighbour and, I'm proud to say, ardent fan. The Shah of Iran lived above me and another neighbour, Nathan Cummings, had a six-million-dollar art collection in his apartment.

Sammy Cahn arranged for me to see this extraordinary collection, and soon I was spending hours at Nathan Cummings' place in the Waldorf Towers, looking at Rodins, Renoirs, and Miller sculptures. He had many more paintings at the Metropolitan Museum of Art. Around dinnertime I told him that art for me had to yield to the prosaic . . . that my cook had already started dinner.

'I wish I could have a home-cooked dinner some time,' he said.

'You can,' I said. 'Just come downstairs.'

Not a man to come to dinner empty-handed, he arrived at my door with a selection of frozen Stouffer's items and heads of lettuce. A man of parts, was Mr Cummings . . .

During my second engagement at Basin Street, we had to turn a lot of people away, and so Phoebe Jacobs prevailed on Capitol to record at the club. I was hesitant. One night Cary Grant was in my dressing room and I was telling him about them wanting me to record at the club. The real problem was, I had a bad cold and didn't want to record at all until I got over it. But when Cary said it was a good idea, I was easily won over. If you listen to the record, *Basin Street East*, you sure can tell I have the cold. It turned out to be a hit, on *Billboard* for forty weeks and still sells today. Maybe I should always sing with a cold – a different sound . . .

Phoebe remembers how I recognized Quincy Jones and Ray Charles before they became famous. 'Miss Lee enquired who arranged for Quincy Jones, and when I told her he did his own, she immediately spoke to him about conducting for her. Later Quincy wrote "New York City Blues" and "Grain Belt Blues" with Miss Lee. And she was the first popular artist to salute Ray Charles. He heard about it and came in to Basin Street East one night. Afterwards he cried in my office and called her "Sister Peggy". Nicki and my daughter, who were good friends, were ardent fans of Ray Charles.'

After a performance I would need to unwind and so I'd take my friends to my apartment for breakfast. Martha Raye, Judy Garland, and Cary Grant would sit around the table while I prepared, among other things, frankfurters or onion sandwiches with champagne. Cary thought hot dogs and champagne were a funny idea but loved the end result. 'A refreshing change from caviar,' Cary said. Who else but Cary Grant could get away with *that* line? One night Ray Charles wanted pizza, so we all took off for pizza. People, all sorts of people, would come back to the Waldorf with me after a show: Benoit Dreyfus, jeweller; Bill Harbach, producer; Bill Mandel from Revlon; Fred Klein, the man of a thousand voices. We'd all march to the Waldorf, singing, and have a good old get-together. I'd take off my gown and get into a hostess outfit and make hotcakes for everyone. One night Charles Revson sent a washtub full of roses.

It really seemed like the whole world was coming to Basin Street East. Phoebe told me Tony Bennett called me from Detroit asking the time of the last show, and asked her to hold a table for him. He made it . . . and Anthony Quinn sent a cable from Europe saying he was coming in . . . and he did. Later Quinn and I made a TV Special together, *A Man and a Woman*. He's wonderful!

I guess you could say the people of New York adopted me during the Basin Street East days. Vinnie Promuto, captain of the Washington Redskins, was always there to help me get through crowds. They had constructed a marquee and had my name up in lights, and the street in front of Basin Street was chaotic. This was a residential area, and mounted police had to be there to handle the crowds. The writers were great to me – Murray Kempton, Albert Goldman, Tommy Thompson – all did big pieces on what was going on at Basin Street East.

Phoebe Jacobs remembers me doing an impression of Billie Holiday for Nat King Cole and Ella Fitzgerald who were in the audience. 'Peggy was singing "God Bless the Child", which Billie wrote. Ralph Watkins, one of the owners, had often booked Billie herself to sing at his previous club, Kelly's Stable. When Ralph heard Peg singing that night, he turned white as a sheet, it was so much like Billie, but of course Billie was already dead. Later Nat King Cole came into my office and cried, saying, "That was Billie." '

The early 1960s were happy, sad days. My business manager of some fifteen years, George Stuart, was suddenly taken ill (while working on my income tax!). His partner, Richard Shipman, and I spent a great deal of time at St John's Hospital, where the neurologist told me, on George's instructions, that he had found cancer of the brain and it was inoperable.

I was so fond of George, it was as though he were a member of my family. I tried my best to help Dick keep him as comfortable as possible, and I delayed the European trip I was due to make until George passed.

Edward Sebesta made a whole wardrobe for my trip to London and Monaco in 1961. I was so happy to be taking my beloved sister Marianne with me as well as my dear Nicki, who promised me she would speak French for me . . . Jim Mahoney was just starting in the press-relations business and while we were flying to New York, I turned to him and said, 'Jim, there's something I forgot to mention.' 'Oh?' 'I want you to go to London with me.' 'Egad,' he said, 'I don't even have my passport in order. I don't have any clothes – ' 'We'll take care of that in New York,' I said very grandly.

I'll always remember Nicki, Marianne, and I standing at the rail of the SS United States with confetti and streamers filling the air and realizing we were leaving the shores of America for the first time; when the ship let out its sonorous ho-o-nk, we all burst into tears. 'Oh, beautiful for spacious skies, for amber waves of grain . . .'

Meyer Davis was the orchestra leader on the ship and Jim Mahoney borrowed a tuxedo from him (a little on the large side). Our first night out, Jim and I were doing the cha-cha and he all but lost his trousers.

There were some lovely passengers aboard. Among those we knew were Estée Lauder and her party, Jackie Gleason and his party; Ann Spalding Hamilton became a new friend. The great movie choreographer Hermes Pan, who guided Rita Hayworth through her musicals, was one of the most delightful people aboard. One night during a hurricane we kept dancing, sliding from one end of the dance floor to the other when the big ship tilted. I said, 'Oh, Hermes, that was *special*.' My hairdresser, Faith Schmerr, had a 'wnnerful, wnnerful' time and the 'morning after' she and I were both sitting on the bathroom floor, she clutching her head and I clutching the bathmat with the eagle holding the sheaves of golden grain in its claws. The crew was passing out motion-sickness pills while she attempted to make me look glamorous. Dinners at the captain's table and in our own private little dining room were delicious. All in all, it was a beautiful voyage and we landed in Southampton, where we caught the boat train for London.

Jim briefed me about the British press before the press conference we had on arrival. It was a champagne brunch, and I was glad he had warned me – I declined the champagne and was able to answer the quick-fire questions. I had a healthy respect for the British press by the time we finished, but I couldn't believe it when we were headlines in the papers: 'PEGGY IS PURRFECT'.

We were chauffeured to the Dorchester and passed Buckingham Palace where I did *not* see the changing of the guard. Meanwhile, Jim Mahoney had radioed his wife Patti to meet him. She was as excited as a new bride, and, of course, with a name like Mahoney, they had to take a trip to Ireland.

I had the Oliver Messel Suite at the Dorchester, one of the most attractive penthouses in the world. When we first entered, Jim pressed some buttons, saying, 'I wonder what these – ' Before he could finish the sentence, maids, butlers and valets popped in from doors, some even, I swear, from behind the bookcase, saying, 'Yes sir, Yes mum.' I murmured to Jim, 'I wonder what you press to get them to go back in again.'

Armsloads of beautiful flowers were brought into the suite and I saw rubrum lilies for the first time. Almost every celebrity had stayed there, most recently Elizabeth Taylor and Richard Burton. It had a terrace that stretched around three sides, with a view of London that was unbeatable. There was one pigeon, one big old pigeon, who used to waddle around the terrace all day waiting for the tea sandwiches – I think he had eaten so many he couldn't fly.

One time, however, we did get homesick. I ordered a chicken pot pie and waiters came up with a battery of silver. I said we would like to serve ourselves, which wasn't really to their liking, but we wanted to feel as though we were at home. I picked up the lid of the big silver pot and there was a little chicken lying there all dressed with its feet in the air holding a piece of parsley. We were listening to an album someone had sent me of Ray Charles singing 'Georgia on My Mind' and as Ray sang 'Georgia, Georgia, no peace I find,' I burst into tears. Isn't it funny how we pick out a spot and say that's my spot? The lovely chintzes, the down-filled couches, the wonderful English decor didn't sooth our mood. It seems like you just want some of your own dirt. (In fact someone sent me some dirt from home in an envelope, and it had a profound effect on me. But of course it could have been from anywhere, you could have fooled me.)

I performed at the Pigalle. It had been sold out for some time in advance. It was such an honour to have Princess Margaret and others of the royal party come to the performance. They laid sheets on the kitchen floor so she could come in through the back entrance.

In addition to the scheduled performances, I was doing television shows, one of which I wrote with Robert Farnum (the dean of British composer-conductors). We got very little sleep, perhaps two hours a night because we had to leave for the television studios in Teddington early in the morning and return in time for the evening performances. When we got back into London, I would lie on the cement floor of a Pigalle dressing room and take a nap, as the people walked above me in Piccadilly Square. I discovered an old spiderwebby closet at the Pigalle: an air-raid shelter from the war. How brave those people were to withstand all of those bombings! We made lots of new friends in London and I found people to be warm and friendly. Each time I go back I especially look forward to seeing Dennis Chappell; we have a nice quiet friendship.

One friend who became sort of a camp-follower was young Lord Rudolph. I think he was seventeen at the time, sensitive and impressionable. He was such a fan that he followed us over to Monaco at the end of our visit in London. At Nice airport we were met by the paparazzi, who followed us everywhere, flashbulbs blazing away. 'LORD RUDOLPH FOLLOWS PEGGY LEE TO FRANCE!' It was an international incident, bigger than 'PEGGY LEE STEALS DOG!' I was pleased to hear that the Duke of Bedford, when questioned, said in effect, 'She is a sensible, sane woman and will know how to handle this.'

We took a helicopter from Nice to Cannes – Moe Lewis, a writer from *Punch* magazine, the musicians from my quartet, my sister Marianne, Faith Schmerr, Nicki and I – and Lord Rudolph. Flying over the Mediterranean gave me one of the scares of my life. I was happily taking in everything I could see, turned to look back at Nicki and noticed *her door was open*. I thought I was going to faint, but instead I yelled at the pilot, who spoke only French. I was pointing back at Nicki, but he didn't understand me and kept nodding his head, *'Oui, merveilleux.'* I was so frightened I don't know how we got that door shut, but Nicki was happy as a clam.

In Cannes the press was there in force, shooting questions above the loud flapping sound of the helicopter. I must have caught a bug in London, because by now I had walking pneumonia. We checked into the Hôtel de Paris and Nicki called the doctor, who told me to go to bed. I spent most of the time in France in bed – alone, of course, although when I tried to order some Pouilly-Fuissé, the waiter tried to jump in bed with me. I must have said something wrong. I'll never forget how Nicki ordered dinner in flawless French, but when answered in machine-gun-like French, she closed her mouth and hasn't spoken a word of French since. Farewell, Madam Egan.

I was well enough to do the gala for Princess Grace and the Red Cross. I was looking forward to seeing the comedian Señor Wenses, who was also performing, and I wasn't disappointed. 'E-e-e-s difficult? No, e-e-e-s easy.'

I remember being fascinated by Aristotle Onassis, the Greek shipping magnate who later married Jackie Kennedy. He and his entourage seemed to wander around like hounds trying to find a little *joie de vivre*. (I later met Jackie and was invited to the Compound. She looked like a frightened fawn, but, obviously, she wasn't. She was a woman of courage.)

With Lord Rudolph we travelled around the French countryside and I was full of the wonder of it all – the smell of French bread, the pungent smell of salami, and wine . . . Lord Rudolph, or Rue, as he asked to be called, was bored and unhappy. Moe would get impatient with him because Moe, too, was trying to get me alone to ask me to marry him.

Dancing under the stars on the Riviera was heady stuff, especially when you had two men taking turns asking you to marry them. The orchestra was playing 'Moanin',' and I couldn't understand that they could play such progressive jazz yet not speak English. Picture me standing in front of the bandstand saying, 'Will you play "Moanin' " again?' They smiled at me. *'Parle pas anglais. Parlez-vous français, mademoiselle?'*

When we came to board the ship for America, everyone began to get misty-eyed. The *Punch* writer decided he wanted to go to America with me, and so did Lord Rudolph. Then the writer discovered his passport had expired the day before! That was all right with me. Rue offered to try to help him, but of course that wouldn't do. Ann Hamilton Spalding came back on board, and Jackie Gleason and his party arrived with photographs and acetates of his film *Gigot*. He told me he was going to arrange for me to hear the acetates and I couldn't wait.

We settled in for the voyage and each night Moe Lewis sent a case of Dom Perignon to my stateroom with instructions to 'get rid' of the case that evening. It became a full-time job passing out the champagne.

The night I went to Jackie's stateroom to hear the music, a stiff wind had come up and become a hurricane. He had arranged with the engineer to fasten the turntable in the centre of the ceiling with four grappling hooks extending from each corner of the room. Jackie kept trying to make his method work but the needle was sliding to the centre of the record and back. It ruined his acetates.

Very soon, signs were up all over the ship warning us to wear topsiders, and ropes were strung so we wouldn't slide over the railing. We were all having a wonderful time and no one was much perturbed by the hurricane except those of us who went to a movie starring George Hamilton: the screen kept sliding back and forth!

Finally we landed, all in one piece. I was scheduled to sing at Basin Street again, with Quincy Jones. He and I had written a number of blues pieces for a Capitol album called *Blues Cross Country*. He was absolutely perfect to work with. Years later, on the famous *We are the World* video, you saw what a fantastic talent he is. There was only one problem. The bug I'd had in France had gotten bigger and soon I was having severe pains in my chest.

One night the pain was too much for me. I had a 103° fever and called Dr Palmer. I was not able to stand up for Dr Palmer to tape me, so he asked Faith Schmerr to hand him the tape. She was so frightened, she taped me to the doctor! My sense of humour never failed. I laughed about a quarter of an inch and then fainted. When I came to Doctor Palmer said, 'Well, this is one you're going to have to miss.' With great effort, I begged, 'Please . . .' 'If you can stand after I tape you, I'll consider it,' he said, thinking it totally impossible. I could stand, but because I couldn't sit down, I *walked*, very slowly, from the Waldorf to Basin Street East, with my car trailing along beside me in case I fell down.

We were sold out as usual, and leaning against a pressing board, I managed through sheer willpower to do two performances. I did begin to faint during the second performance and was barely able to signal Quincy Jones that they should jump to the final song.

The ambulance men were so gentle. 'Yeah, Peg – you're gonna be all right . . .'

It was double pneumonia in both lungs plus pleurisy. They sent for Nicki.

At a critical point in the illness, Dr Palmer called in Dr Daniel Mulvihill, chief-of-staff at St Vincent's Hospital in New York City. I don't really know what procedure was used. My body was distended an unbelievable amount. There were six or seven doctors. Doctor Mulvihill put a wide strip of adhesive tape around me, and as he looked deep into my eyes and quickly pulled on the tape, everything in front of me disappeared. I left this earthly plane for a few seconds but was given the choice of returning.

Many people have asked me to describe my out-of-body experience, and since it made me comfortable with my own self, I decided it would be all right to include it. From my position in the bed, I went up and straight ahead, then turned to look down at myself on the bed from that vantage point. There was no body, only consciousness. The pain was gone and a deep sense of serenity followed. Suddenly, I could see everywhere at once. I saw all of the doctors from their back as well as their front. I saw to the right, to the left and to the back of me at once. I saw me in pain, and somehow was given the opportunity of re-entering my body. It was all light. I was made to understand that if I returned, the pain would return, but I could go on if I wished. All fear was gone.

It was an enlightening experience for which I am very grateful.

Basin Street East closed for several days while I was on the critical list. Then followed seven months in bed.

I came back to years of pain, but with the wonderful help of Dr John Jones, I more than survived.

7

The Folks Who Live On The Hill

I went back to Kimridge Road to recover from the pneumonia. Sometimes the clouds would float over the swimming pool and I would lie on the island looking up at the sky and listen to the beautiful music coming from the outside speakers – or maybe it was heaven! I used to sneak out into my private garden and paint there. Oh, I loved that place . . .

While I spent all those months in bed after my double pneumonia, Frank Sinatra did something wonderful every day on his way down the hill to see Nancy and the children: he would bring lovely flowers, lots of lilacs, lots of roses; a book he found interesting; an album I would enjoy; an Aztec wood carving; and when he was away there were telephone calls to see how I was feeling. A crew arrived and installed extra air conditioning in my bedroom because he heard the heat was bothering me. A truck arrived with barbecues and flares or torches to stick in the ground and at the barbecue he personally served Murray Wolf and me because we were the 'invalids'.

And now it was the 1960s. A decade for me of shock and celebration.

When Ernest Holmes died in 1960, it shook me up so much I was going to leave New York and come out to Los Angeles for the funeral and cancel a Revlon show. I called Adela Rogers St John, whom I'd met at Ernest's old house on Third and Lorraine in LA. 'Adela, what should I do?'

'You stay here,' she said. 'That's what Ernest would want you to do. Let's arrange a memorial service here.' Adela got me to sing 'The Lord's Prayer' at Ernest's memorial, which was held in New York's Town Hall.

Adela told me she often prayed for me. 'Expect the best,' she would say, 'and it will come.' I do believe it is true that we are capable of doing powerful 'treatments' for each other.

(When Louis Armstrong died, his widow Lucille also asked me to sing 'The Lord's Prayer', at Satchmo's funeral. I loved both Louis and Lucille very much and went over to Queens for the funeral. At the service I was a little nervous. It's hard to sing at a friend's funeral. There were newsreel cameras going. I just kept looking at Louis in his open casket. The man, his music, are eternal.)

It was President Kennedy's birthday. I suppose he was almost everybody's idol and I was eager to accept the invitation to sing for his big birthday party at the Madison Square Garden, though my doctor was not ready to give me permission. He was worried enough that I had gone back to work so soon after the frightening illness and was doing three shows a night. In the end Dr Palmer didn't exactly give me permission; he just gave up. He couldn't quite believe that I was still alive and finally just threw up his hands. 'Well, if she goes, she goes.'

So I went over to the Garden with the musicians and my light man, Hugo Granata. (Dinah Shore and a couple of other luminous stars used him too, but I worked with him so steadily, I liked to think of him as 'my man'.) There was a buzz of excitement, the place fairly crackling with electricity. Hugo did his usual wonderful lighting set up. He always did a lot of back lighting and would warn me to take proper precautions with my gowns – in other words, to have the gowns lined or wear a slip.

During the rehearsal the producer of the event told Hugo that Marilyn Monroe was coming and she would sing 'Happy Birthday' to J.F.K. Would Hugo do her lights? He asked if I minded, and I said, 'Of course not, go ahead.' I remember I was arguing with a security man who kept telling me my band was too loud, and I was defending them – while asking them to play softer. But they were like race horses ready to burst out of the gate. They couldn't wait to play for the President. I don't think they minded Marilyn Monroe either.

Marilyn was on before me. She walked out on to the stage as the lights went up full. The whole audience gasped, and I thought it was just Marilyn's charisma, but as I turned to look I gasped too. She had *nothing* on under a sheer gown: she looked stark naked! Well, I guess she was, except for a little chiffon. No wonder the audience gasped. There was a whole lot of shouting going on from the press and the photographers. It's a good thing 'Happy Birthday' is such a short song.

I finally got to sing Frank Loesser's 'I Believe in You' and a couple of others, but somehow I don't think it mattered. I had been told I was the President's favourite singer, but we had to rush back to Basin Street East for the next show and missed the invitation to the private reception. Every night was like New Year's Eve at Basin Street East.

David and I had a wonderful wedding for Nicki and Dick Foster. People came from all over. Everyone was so fond of both David and Nicki and it seemed proper that we were together.

Since it was a church wedding and the reception was at Kimridge, I got my florist business going again. Of course, Nicki being my only child, and a daughter at that, made this event extra special.

I made two swans out of chrysanthemums, each five feet long. My helpers were my sister Marianne and Robert Preston. We had a large champagne fountain at the centre of the tent with ropes of flowers coming down from the ceiling.

David had quite a time keeping from laughing at himself in tails. He had a silly grin on his face as though he were walking outside of himself and seeing himself – he was not the tails type.

Oh, how true that empty-nest syndrome is!

> The room was pale yellow
> And frothy and white
> The room was pale yellow
> And full of light
> The bridal veil was tossed on the bed –
> The flowers were fading
> And I – looked ahead
>
> My little girl has gone away
> All grown up and she's gone away
> Married and all with the ring and the rice
> Everything's tidy – and proper – and nice
>
> We did it all with the little white glove
> Engraved invitations and champagne and love
> Every detail was refined to the bone
> The house is now empty
> And I – I'm alone

My little girl has gone away
All grown up and she's gone away
Married and all with the ring and the rice
Everything tidy and proper . . .
And nice

When Nicki got married we sold Kimridge Road and I moved to a penthouse in a brand-new apartment building. It looked like a movie set, but I was absolutely paranoid about living there – up on the thirteenth floor, open all around, alone after everyone had gone home for the day – because I used to walk in my sleep. I was afraid I'd walk out the window.

We gave a big party there, hoping to break the lease. At some point we put on my new recording of 'Pass Me By' from *Father Goose*, which Cy Coleman had just finished scoring. We played it at full volume and marched down the hall, into the elevator, continuing to march in place, outside into the lobby, around the lobby, back into the elevator and back upstairs to the penthouse.

Cary Grant, who was the guest of honour, was the drum major; I wore some Indian footbells; Cy was a couple of trombones at least. Unfortunately, the landlord didn't break the lease; he loved the excitement. Inevitably, I moved out anyway and bought a house on Tower Grove Drive, which is about when Cary began seeing Dyan Canon. He couldn't wait to have a child. After Jennifer was born they would come to my house and Cary would play with her on the floor. He worshipped her.

I once sang 'Mr Wonderful' to Cary over the balcony at the Waldorf-Astoria. He liked that. It was his birthday, and during rehearsal for the grand bash the Friars Club was giving for him, I decided to sing to him down there on the dais from the balcony.

It's so difficult to think of a world without Cary Grant, so I think I'll just remember the last time I actually saw him. He and Barbara came to the Westwood Playhouse with Gregory and Veronique Peck and Robert Wagner with Jill St John. After the performance, he stood and smiled at me for the longest time, with the most special look of affection I've ever seen. I had no idea it would be the last, for now at least.

After my grandson David was born Nicki and Dick came to live in my penthouse and then moved with me to Tower Grove Drive. It was 1965, and David and I were discussing the possibility of remarrying. He believed he could handle it because he had been sober for thirteen years. Four days later David was dead. It was a terrible shock to me and to all of our friends.

I remember an amusing incident concerning Kathy Levy, my new hairdresser, who became a long-time friend. Helen Glickstein, Dr Jonas Salk's cousin, and I presented a gala for the Salk Institute at the Empire Room of the Waldorf-Astoria. It was an auspicious gala. Dave Garroway, the master of ceremonies for us for the evening, was brilliant, as usual. He pointed out that polio had been so thoroughly put down by Dr Salk's vaccine that young people, whose lives may well have been saved by the vaccine, don't remember him. I came running off stage from my bows in the Empire Room – I had only seconds to powder my nose, drink something and touch up my lips. Kathy was holding a glass of Coca-Cola for me but I fell down the ramp and knocked her flat – Coke spilling in my hair. When assured she was all right, I ran back on stage again as though nothing had happened, but I suppose the audience must have wondered, 'Why did she run all the way off stage to get her eyelashes and hair wet?' Fortunately they dried quickly in the spotlight although one eyelash had a rakish angle to it. That little baby, named David, is over six feet tall now . . .

One of the door prizes at the gala was a little black poodle, named Stanley by my niece Merrilee. He had been left behind by a couple of guests who after a little bit too much champagne, had forgotten him. When I finally found them and told them I had gotten rather attached to the dog, they said, 'Well, keep him.' There was a limit to the number of dogs I could have in California, so I wound up giving the dog to restaurateur Bruce Vanderhoff . . .

I'd been commissioned by Sylvania Company to do four paintings for an enormous advertising campaign on the subject 'The Sights and Sounds of the 1970s'. If you recall, that was a period when the word 'pollution' was on everyone's mind. Looking for a positive approach, I painted fields of flowers, and fresh lemons in the sunshine, two oranges kissing each other, and I wanted to paint a chicken – the egg, I thought, was the symbol of new life and hope. The other paintings of the flowers and fruit were faring well, but the chicken was not, so one evening I sat at the end of my living room with five canvases and started furiously painting chicken feathers. After I decided on red wattles, I thought he must be a rooster. How could he have possibly laid that egg on the table next to him? Finally, I took a nice wide brush and swept it across the canvas. Now the chicken was standing in a bowl and his legs were sticking out the bottom as though a pedestal for the bowl. Don't you know the men from Sylvania wanted to buy that painting? But I wouldn't let them. About 200,000 of the other prints were sold, but the chicken hangs in my living room today behind a potted palm. It looks so purposeful, as if to say, 'I dare you to say anything about that egg.'

I was proud to be awarded a doctorate from the University of North Dakota. I went back to North Dakota to receive it and, of course, it was a beautiful, sentimental trip; I saw so many old friends. Ken Kennedy was still alive. What a joy it was to spend time with him and his wife Jeanette, as well as with Sev Olson and his wife.

In 1976, after Ken's death, *The Sunday Forum Fargo-Moorehead* printed a tribute I had written as part of a memorial column dedicated to him: 'I know I'm only one of so many, many people who feel the great loss of this wonderful man. My whole life would be so much different – so much less fulfilled – but for this dear friend . . . He was responsible for nurturing my career; for changing my name; teaching me; advising me; being my friend always. If ever I needed help – and there were many times – he was always there, he and his dear wife, Jeanette. I will always see his smile, hear his voice, his laugh, feel his understanding and compassion – for he is not gone, nor will he ever be. Part of me will always be a part of him. I'll see you, "kiddo". You are surely in our Father's special care.'

Tower Grove Drive was a beautiful new house surrounded by spectacular pine trees. There was a profusion of geraniums, wild strawberries and some lovely rock garden plants strategically placed around the two pools – the larger pool washing over the rocks to the wading pool. I was enjoying the smell of fresh grass being cut by Hugo, our gardener, when he said, with his Spanish accent, 'Miss Lee, Miss Lee, there's a crack over here on the side of the hill.' I had always lived on granite so I really didn't pay any attention. 'Oh really? Well, maybe you could just fill it in.'

'I did that, but it came back. You'd better come and look.' Yes, it was a rather long crack, but the hillside was large, covered with Algerian ivy.

'Well, Hugo, can't you just fill that up and plant something there?'

'OK, but you'd better watch this all the time. I know a crack when I see one.'

He filled it – it came back, he filled it – it came back. He showed me again, and we began to look at each other warily. 'This crack isn't kidding,' I said. The fence on the side had begun pulling an inch or two away from the house. One day Sungyi La was able to get through it. Big Sur, my big standard poodle, couldn't make it, of course. Not yet . . .

Until now landslides had just been something I saw on the evening news or read in the paper, not something that could happen to me. The crack was extending all along the side of the house where Nicki and her family were living. There began a couple of years of sleepless nights. Nicki probably wasn't sleeping either, but we skirted any talk of the crack.

And then it began to rain. It was one of those times of extended rainfall that broke all records. It rained endlessly, sometimes just sprinkling, broken by an occasional cloudburst. I wasn't paying much attention to the flooding they kept talking about, but I had zeroed in on landslides and the endless soaking rain. All through the night I would imagine, or perhaps it wasn't my imagination, the cracking in the house. I thought of all kinds of rationalizations, like this is a pretty new house, it's just settling. It *was* settling, but not in the way I thought.

Hugo smelled gas, and we immediately called the gas company. We found newspapers stuffed in a gas pipe under the sidewalk right under Nicki's window. That could have blown us all to bits!

One morning I went around the side of the house. Oh, my God! The hill had left the house and was mostly down on Tower Grove Drive!

Hill or no hill, I had to leave for Las Vegas, only to learn that rats had been living under the ivy on the hill; they now invaded every room of the house. They even ate the corners off some of my books and stationery. Between shows in Vegas each night I'd get a report from Nicki about the rats. Johnny Mandel, bless him, went over with some cyanide pellets. I had to move Nicki and the children out of the house, fast, so I rented a couple of bungalows at the Beverly Hills Hotel for them.

By the time I got home, the big caterpillars had arrived to rebuild the hill. I had to get huge wooden containers and rent space at another site for the big pine trees; then the caterpillars started hauling away the dirt, while the rain poured on.

I think my grandson Michael got his love of trucks and caterpillars then. He was just a baby and seemed to never tire of watching them go up and down that hill.

Later I established what had happened. The previous owners had had a landslide, which broke their gas pipe beneath the hill. They scooped it all up and planted Algerian ivy very close together. California law states that you must tell prospective buyers of any such landslide or fault, but the newspapers stuffed in the gas pipe was proof they intended to ignore it all. There was no doubt it was fraud and we had to sue. They counter-sued my attorney Ludwig Gerber and myself for harassment with intent to commit murder! The very word 'murder' makes me shiver. Who was murdering whom? What about the newspaper in the gas pipe?

By the time the hill was rebuilt with steel and reinforced concrete, it was far stronger than it had ever been and all feelings were assuaged. We replaced the trees but to get some new growth planted in a hurry, we shot marigold seeds into the hillside with a special gun. Soon, the whole hillside was covered in orange blooms.

One day a tour bus stopped on its trip up the hill for the passengers to admire the marigolds. They picked quite a few, but what amused me was that two repair trucks were sent to move the tour bus, which had over-heated. One truck was attached to each end of the bus, but they got their signals crossed and pulled the bus right in half! The passengers, all gaily carrying marigolds, had to be transported back down the hill.

We had swimming parties, barbeques and music rehearsals at Tower Grove Drive. Jack Lemmon, our neighbour across the canyon, told me he used to enjoy the music coming out of the hill. One time the music was for a rehearsal of a Julie Andrews special and she asked me if I would like to ride to work with her in her helicopter. What a wonderful way to go to work. Since I lived very near her, I gladly accepted. I would have anyway. She has always been fascinating to me, as to millions of others.

I asked Julie if we could fly over Nicki's house in Cheviot Hills. I wanted to drop something on the roof for the children, and she agreed. So, I lugged a giant, six-foot, plastic bag of rose petals that I had been saving into the kitchen to see if they would fit in the helicopter. You see, every week a silent lover sent me six dozen roses, so I had plenty of petals! I wonder what happened to him.

Just to walk into the entrance of Julie's beautiful home and through to the kitchen was an experience. There was something very elegantly homey about it – the smell of coffee and toast – and hearing her call up the grand staircase, 'Blake . . . Blackie, are you there?' That lovely English accent.

We chatted away as we drove to the Bank of America Building – a little about the show, a bit about Bill Harbach and Bill Davis, who were producing and directing, and about what a marvellous crew we had. When we were there, she took me via a kind of secret route to the elevator that led up to the roof. By George! Maybe she *was* Mary Poppins (I felt like Little Bo Peep). We crawled up into the copter and she proceeded to unwrap the map of the area. Nicki and I had arranged to have a bright red beach towel on the roof as a marker. Julie sat in front with the pilot. I sat in the back with my huge bag of rose petals. We took off from the roof. Over the roar and rattle of the helicopter I heard her direct the pilot: 'Turn left no, turn right, hold it just a moment. Peggy, do we go this way?' pointing a finger.

'Please, don't ask me; I get lost in my own driveway. Look for the red beach towel; they said they'd have it – '

'There! I see something red.' And to the pilot, 'Over there, please. See that red? that's it, that's it.' She called to me, 'Now, open up now, toss them out! Now!' I wrestled with the bag and pushed the petals out of the copter. They looked so beautiful . . . a shower of rose petals falling down, down, down.

On the wrong house!

The show won an Emmy, and Julie and I, joined by Peter Ustinov, went on to do a Christmas special in England.

In 1970 I decided to keep my fiftieth birthday a secret, but gave a big party and invited 100 guests to come dressed as clowns. We had the entire back garden covered with a circus tent, and I rented all manner of circus accessories, such as peanut and popcorn wagons.

We had calliope music as well as a loop-tape of Barnum and Bailey circus marches. What a show!

No one recognized Hermes Pan and Rita Hayworth, who won the first prize for the classic clown. Rita was a frequent guest in my home. A charming woman. Her daughter Princess Yasmin is active in the Women's International Centre, an organization working for peace, and later I would receive their Living Legacy Award, presented to me by Dr Jonas Salk. A real thrill. Much as I liked Rita Hayworth, I thought my sister should have won. Atop her rosy cheeks and putty nose, she had a miniature derby, with a daisy standing straight and tall in the air. I was a lion with ostrich plumes wrapping my head for the mane. The judge, a real-life judge, came dressed as the devil. Clay, now my road manager and lighting director, came dressed as the tin-man clown, courtesy of Paul Galbraith, who does those fantastic paper sculptures on television. The cake, of course, was a circus. It was a super night. And I was fifty.

You've heard about accompanists that try to steal the show . . . Well, it was the afternoon of a large, important gala. I'm talking Texas large. The immense ballroom was filled with what seemed to be hundreds of tables. There were clusters of waiters busying themselves with laying the linens, and the florists bringing in a profusion of colourful flowers. From where I stood, the room looked like a haze of very pale blue linen with flashes of coral, white, pink, yellow, green and blue flowers. They left a ring in the centre of each table, perhaps for some kind of candle centrepiece, I thought. I turned my attention to the rehearsal. My conductor asked me a few technical questions, and then we were about to begin.

Suddenly, way down at the end of the ballroom, the doors burst open and a team of men came through carrying pale blue bird cages, each with a pale blue bird inside: a bird in a cage for each table. Texans really do things up proud! And the cages were tall, slim, delicately wrought like Dufy cages.

The orchestra was tuning. It was time for me to sing. My conductor nodded. About three or four notes into the first song, the birds began. Just a few – then more and more of them. I stopped. They stopped. I began again. They began again.

I thought, 'Well, I guess they like music.' The orchestra played the instrumental segment of the song, and the birds just listened. I tried again – they followed me. My God! What am I going to do? They want to sing with *me*!

After a half-dozen tries, we were convinced that, left to their own, they would, indeed, sing with me. At first I thought it was a compliment, but after a while I wasn't sure. We had a conference with the florists and the management. As long as the birds didn't sing while the orchestra played, they could sit in the centre of the table. When my performance began they would be removed to an adjoining ballroom, where they would stay while I sang.

We were backstage while the thousand or more guests were having a fabulous evening. There was some chirping here and there, but it all blended with the laughter and conversation, the clinking of glasses, the clanking of silver. After dinner, on cue, the florist removed all the birds from the tables (I imagine the guests were puzzled), and they were all closed up in the room next door. I heaved a sigh: all was well. The orchestra began the overture, they announced my name and I made my entrance.

I began to sing.

The birds heard me through the wall and began to sing with me. Those birds had great ears – great 'back-up' singers.

At Tower Grove Drive on New Year's Eve the guest list read: Rudolf Nureyev, Margot Fonteyn, the Fifth Dimension, the Florida Cowans, Bob and Dorothy Mitchum, Victoria and Ed McMahon, Cary Grant, Bobby Darin, Mia Farrow, Laurence Harvey, Margaret Whiting, Tony Bennett, Andy Williams, a number of my doctor friends, Natalie Wood, Bob Wagner, Quincy Jones, Shirley MacLaine, and Helen Glickstein came from New York to surprise me. We put the sound system all through the house and we all sang 'Auld Lang Syne' until the house fairly lifted off the hill.

I really don't know what tells me to sell a house – maybe I wanted to find another house to decorate – and I found a little jewel box up on Blue Jay Way in the Doheney Hills. It was so tiny that my dog Genghis and I lived alone there for a while. Lloyd and James, Lillie Mae and Virginia, had all worked for me up on Tower Grove Drive, but I couldn't bring them to live in because there was only room in a little guest house which I had not yet furnished. It began to bother me that you could see right into the house from outside, but Genghis was such a good guard dog that one night he would not go to sleep until I put on the security system. I've never figured out just how he could tell the difference between the red and green lights. I thought dogs were colour blind.

The view from Blue Jay Way was spectacular, right up there with all those birds, and reminded me of the property that I had bought with David, and I wondered how life would have been if he hadn't sold it. Would we have built a home up there? Still, no use crying over spilled money. I was sort of restless in the house, so I went to Detroit with the Stephen Sondheim company to do *Side by Side by Sondheim*. It was fun and I enjoyed getting to know what it would be like in real theatre.

We were rehearsing one day in the theatre and during a little intermission Paul Horner, one of the accompanists, was playing a beautiful melody. I called to him, 'What is that Paul?' 'It's mine,' he said. I walked over. 'Does that have lyrics?' 'No, I was hoping you might want to write some.'

I began writing immediately. I could hear the title in his music: 'I Gave It Everything I Had'. The cast came on stage again after the break and we played it for them right then and there. They were very encouraging, and urged us to keep on writing.

Paul Horner's dream and mine was to write a Broadway show, and that was how the idea for *Peg* was born.

Back in LA, after making a few improvements to the house on Blue Jay Way, I sold it, to a very happy tenant. Out house hunting (again) with Genghis, we rounded a corner on Bellagio Drive and I said, 'That house.' Genghis was shivering with excitement – I guess he knew in advance too. The realtor said, 'No, that's not on the market.' I had gone through many houses in the Bel Air/Beverly Hills area, but none had attracted me as much as this place. The owner was an Iranian, and somehow I talked him into selling me the house.

Some of my friends thought I was foolish, but I could see the house all renovated and shining. It was a beautiful French Regency with a two-storey foyer. From the ceiling hangs a huge eighteenth-century crystal chandelier. Genghis immediately chose his place of honour from which to welcome guests: directly under the chandelier.

The first thing I decided to do was to repair the mansard roof, and paint the rooms different shades of peach, apricot, and nude, leaving the cornices white. The office, the studio, the kitchen should be white lacquer; every vegetable or piece of fruit would then be an accent piece.

It was so much fun to decorate the house. Bruce Vanderhoff, who owns Le Restaurant, was a big help. He found a magnificent mirror that just fitted on the mantle in the living room, wonderful marble and etched glass, and supplied an entire crew of craftsmen. My major domo José Prado and his family have had a great part in the refurbishing of this house and continue to keep everything fresh and beautiful. I think they must feel they have part of it, and they do.

When I came here, I only knew I felt at home. And that seems to be one of the things I've looked for all my life. There's something about this place that is conducive to writing and painting. My daughter Nicki has become an artist, doing watercolours and poin-tillist paintings. I admire her work so much that I decided to stop painting – mothers and daughters shouldn't have too much competition. Her first big West Coast exhibition was a great success, and perhaps when she is established as the fine artist she is, I'll try my hand at it again.

In 1976 I went on a concert tour to Japan. I was also representing the US at the Mitsukoshi Department Store's celebration of our bicentennial. Mitsukoshi made bronze busts of four of our presidents and they had Max Factor make dress forms to fit all the gowns worn by all the presidents' wives. The gowns, from the Helen Larson collection, were truly lovely.

We took the bullet train to a magnificent man-made lake surrounded by castles that were copies of famous European castles. While we were at the lake we saw *Swan Lake* and then there was the most fantastic fireworks display as the symphony orchestra played the 1812 overture. Some of the fireworks were actually under water. Imagine the beauty of a Japanese night, the giant pines witnessing it all, the magnificent ballet, the beautiful music . . . And then the orchestra played 'Stars and Stripes For Ever'; it's no wonder we all cried.

I began painting fabric designs for Mitsukoshi. Everything and everyone was so lovely, except for one ride in a 747, coming from Sapporo and Osaka to Tokyo in a typhoon. I had the first of many heart spells just before we hit the typhoon. I was on the floor and the Japanese aboard were taking such conscientious care of me, that

I was soaking wet from all the damp cloths and ice cubes. By the time we reached Tokyo I had to be taken out a side door.

We did many concerts there and were all so warmly received that I hated to leave.

The next year we decided to travel to London and I was invited to sing at the Royal Command performance for the Queen Mother's birthday. The other performers included Larry Hagman, Mary Martin, James Cagney, Pat O'Brien, Aretha Franklin, Victor Borge, Sammy Davis and Henry Mancini.

I continued to have fibrillations and more than once had to call Dr McEachens and have him listen to my pacer tracer. From London I went on to Amsterdam and stayed in the Presidential Suite at the Amsterdam Hilton, where I had to call a doctor to help us assemble my IPP Bennett respirator. Ever since I'd had double pneumonia my lung had needed from three to five treatments a day, so I always travelled with two of these machines, which I nicknamed 'Charlie'. That doctor had the biggest handlebar moustache I have ever seen. It extended a good six or seven inches on either side of his nose. Very successfully waxed, it flapped as he talked. Jerry Powell, my musician on keyboards, and I found it very difficult to keep from laughing, although this was quite a serious matter.

(Sometime during the next year or two, I gave up 'Charlie' – my lung was better, so I gratefully passed the two machines off to the American Lung Association. Doctor Jones had originally said, 'You might as well buy these, Peggy. Most people who have this condition don't live very long.' He must have scared me into getting well.)

In Amsterdam I played at the Vieux Carré. It was a magnificently appointed theatre but it was so cold in the dressing room I had to wear my mink while putting on my make-up. At that point I was told that royalty would be attending, so, shivering with the cold, I started practising a proper introduction. But every time I tried to say, 'Her Royal Highness Princess Marguerite and Prince Phillip Von Volenhauven,' it came out, 'Her Royal Harness'! And wouldn't you know, I said that on stage as well. Fortunately they were a charming couple, and I was astounded to learn they were fans.

I returned to the US to sing with the symphony at Walnut Creek near San Francisco. After my heart and lung problems my resistance was down and I was struck with a 105° fever. I barely remember singing that evening and only babbled as we flew home. We called

Dr Jaime Paris, who told them to pack me in ice and bring me to the hospital. I was desperately ill and was told that I had a heart condition, diabetes, and Ménière's disease, a disorder of the inner ear. I went blind temporarily.

When you're blind you wander around feeling walls and familiar furniture like you've never known them. The worst feeling was when I felt paralysis coming over one whole side of my face, like a claw had hold of it and was twisting it into a grimace. When the paralysis came, the sight went too. I could *feel* the terrible expression as my face twisted, and I avoided every mirror in the room when my sight returned. I would walk holding my IV stand, which I called Fred. One day I accidentally saw my paralysed face. I was horrified and wouldn't move. My therapist Fran Owen worked daily on that for hours at a time, during which sessions the neighbours, I was told, could hear me screaming.

Still almost blind, I promptly booked myself into Australia, Orlando, Florida, and everywhere else I could. Fran Owen travelled with me; she pulled me back together. Saved me from falling off the stage in Australia – 'Stop,' she'd say, or 'turn right,' as I tried to make my way off the stage. In Orlando my friend Pat Shelton saw me walk straight into the lights. I was still partially paralysed on the right side of my face and nearly blind.

The doctors told me I must retire. I said, 'Retire and wait for what?' Dr Richard Barton, Dr Paris, and Dr McEachens all concurred. They were right of course, but I was too stubborn. I had a little more work to do and a lot more wisdom to gather. The doctors kindly said, 'All right, we'll try to help you as much as we can.' And they have.

8

Is That All There Is?

Over the years since Paul Horner and I met in Detroit, in between engagements, we had been writing songs for a Broadway show – thirty in all. When the score was finally finished, we began having backers' dinners at my house, served magnificently by Le Restaurant. At first, we were just more or less auditioning people for the songs and we were delighted with their reaction. Then one night Marge Cowan and I were giving a birthday party for Irv Cowan and people said, 'Sing the score.' I happily complied. Elizabeth Taylor was there with Zev Bufman, and the waiters could hardly keep their minds on the dinner. It was during the time she and Richard Burton were doing *Private Lives* on Broadway. I'll always remember how Danny Thomas jumped up and said, 'I'll give $250,000.' Naïvely, I hadn't had the show backing in mind. It snowballed from there: the Cowans and Zev Bufman wanted to back the play for Broadway.

PEG

Score by Paul Horner and Peggy Lee

Creative Consultant:	Cy Coleman
Director:	Robert Drivas
Executive Assistant:	Victoria Lang
Costume Designer:	Florence Klotz
Costume Execution:	Barbara Matera
Set Design:	Tom H. John
Lighting:	Thomas Skelton
Musical Director:	Larry Fallon
The Rose:	Nicki Lee Foster

Backup Singers

First Soprano:	Mary Sue Barry
Second Soprano:	Doris Eugenio
Alto:	Rose Marie Jun
Tenor:	Brian Quinn
Tenor:	Steve Clayton
Strings:	Ellen McLain
	D. Michael Heath

MISS PEGGY LEE

Arrangers

Artie Butler	Bill Holman
Billy May	Gordon Jenkins
Johnny Mandel	Don Sebesky
Tore Zito	Larry Wilcox
Philip Lang	

Sound: Scott
Sound Consultant: Phil Ramon
Production Photographer: Martha Swope

Orchestra Members
The Quartet

Piano: Mike Renzi
Drums: Grady Tate
Bass: Jay Leonhart
Guitar: Bucky Pizzarelli

Reeds

Ralph Olsen	Ed Salkin
Andy Drelies	Frank Perowsky
Joe Temperley	

Trumpets	Trombones
John Frosk	Harry Divito
Brian O'Flaherty	Sy Berger
Frank Fighera	Tommy Mitchell

French Horns

Doug Norris
Fred Griffen

Guitar: John Basie
Percussion: Joe Passaro
Synthesizer: Lou Forestieri

Strings

Lou Ann Montesi	Winterton Garvey
Amaura Giannini	Abe Appleman
Richard Henrickson	Bruce Berg
Stanley Hunte	Valerie Collymore

Celli

Avron Coleman	Zela Terry

It took a long time to get to the point of the *Playbill* lineup. For a year we worked with such people as Bill Luce, the playwright (*The Belle of Amherst*, which starred Julie Harris), Danya Krupska, choreographer, director Bob Kalfin. As happens sometimes, they

164

were all changed, and finally we worked with Cy Coleman (*Sweet Charity*) and Bobby Drivas. Cy was a child prodigy who's never stopped being brilliant. Bobby Drivas was an actor-director who chewed gum constantly, his handsome, clean jaw-line working away. One day I bought the cast and crew packages of gum and we were *all* chewing away when rehearsal resumed, imitating Bobby. He didn't even notice, he was so busy chewing. (Recently Bobby tragically died of AIDS.)

When the show was due to open, Holly, my granddaughter, who has grown into a beautiful and talented young lady and a wonderful companion for laughing and crying in all the right places, made the move to New York with me. We leased Bellagio Road to some very nice tenants and, in exchange, leased a brand new apartment in New York. It had a great view of the East River from five rooms. Phoebe Jacobs, my old friend from Basin Street East, went shopping for furniture with Holly and me, and we very soon had it looking smart.

We started rehearsing *Peg* in New York at the Minskoff and then the Michael Bennett Studios. It was a whole new world for me. I learned to respect and admire all those people who work on shows; I would see them day after day, the air filled with sounds of counting tempos, dancing, singing. Sometimes I'd take Genghis with me; he looked so tiny in that huge rehearsal hall, but he'd communicate with me from one end to the other, and he loved to share my Granola bars.

Somehow Paul Horner and I had lost the simplicity we had going in LA, but not our friendship. Actually, by now, you could hardly recognize it as the same show. The Cowans and Zev Bufman had brought in two new partners, producers Georgia and Dominic Frontiere. One night Zev Bufman took me to see Cecely Tyson in *The Corn is Green* at the Lunt-Fontanne. I had no idea what he had in mind. *Private Lives* with Elizabeth Taylor and Richard Burton had closed early there, which left Zev with about thirteen months to go on the two-year lease, so he told me I must play that huge theatre. No matter if the dressing room was many floors up and they had to build a bathroom upstairs (I hope someone enjoys it). I couldn't walk up the stairs so they had to install an elevator too.

There was no proper advertising before the show opened. I asked many times when we would be opening so I could get some theatre groups going. I asked David Powers, our press agent, when I could start promoting the show with disc jockeys. He had no answer. By now, *The Corn is Green* had closed and we were in the theatre for rehearsals. I didn't see any marquee going up on the theatre and it never did! On 20 November 1983 in the Sunday *New York Times* there was a full-page ad listing the *wrong* telephone number (if you called it, you simply didn't get an answer). Also, 'Theatre Guide', the paper's free listing, did not run a listing on the same day as our big ad! I'm *sure* if it had been the *Times*' mistake, they would have corrected it. The Ash LeDonne advertising agency had a beautiful poster (which incidentally Nicki and I designed, but the posters were never distributed). Ever since our opening in New York I'm told they have been leaking out of some warehouse and are for sale in some shops as collector's items.

We began preview on 1 December 1983, to open on 14 December, which is probably as bad a time as we could find to open in New York City, especially with no advertising. It was bleak and slushy and cold. I kept hearing the phrase 'tax loss' and wondered what it meant.

But the excitement was growing, at least for me, and I think for Paul Horner and the inner core of the faithful. H. L. Wade, a fan for many years, flew in from San Francisco, as did Dr Hutcherson and his wife Gail, my dentist Dr Stone and his guest. Suddenly there it was, opening night, beautiful flowers everywhere.

When I walked out on the stage I could feel something like cold steel pressing on me, a precognition of the devastating reviews. As a last stroke of genius, our press agent had sent in drama critics – for a *musical*! Technically it may not have been musical because we didn't have any dancers, but with twenty odd songs and a magnificent orchestra and chorus, it should definitely have had music critics.

Three days after opening Irv Cowan said, 'Tomorrow is your last show.' That was so shocking it didn't even get through to me. We determined to be brave and hoped for a miracle. I called Greg Bautzer, my lawyer and an old friend, to see if he could help me get some more money, if that was the problem. He said he would get right back to me and I called the Waldorf to tell the Cowans, only to find they had already left for Florida: they weren't going to be there for the closing performance. Who would put up further backing under such circumstances?

I was so proud of my daughter and granddaughter. They almost held back the tears when the house – packed, despite the reviews – was told, 'This is our closing performance.' Grady Tate made an unscheduled speech to the audience that was truly eloquent. Mike Renzi, Jay Leonhart, Bucky Pizzarelli and the other orchestra members fought back the tears during the forty-five minute standing ovation, the audience cheering us on to keep the show going. The producers never heard that. The final blow was when they threatened to put me in jail for taking my own music home for safety reasons! Holly and Nicki and I, hugging each other and crying, went back to our apartment, where we spent a very bleak Christmas. I thought my heart was broken, and maybe it was.

One of the stars on the team of arrangers for *Peg* was Johnny Mandel. Johnny once told me he 'scored the scenery' in Big Sur when he wrote the music for the movie *The Sandpiper*. It's magnificent scenery and a beautiful score. I've worn out perhaps six tapes and several albums of it. I carry that and Delius' 'On Hearing the First Cuckoo in Spring' whenever I travel. Johnny had sent me a pencil-lead sheet (the very first draft) of 'The Shadow of Your Smile', which he wrote for *The Sandpiper*. Before I could even turn around, everyone had recorded it. I was so disappointed until Johnny called and told me the publisher had given it out, but he had a new song he wanted me to write a lyric for. I was so glad to see him – I was really fond of Johnny. We sat down and played the melody and the lyric 'The Shining Sea' began to dance around in my mind. It was finished in less than an hour.

Johnny looked at me in astonishment. 'How did you do that?'
'Do what?'
'Write those lyrics so fast? Did you know you wrote what's in the film?'
'No . . . what film?'
'*The Russians are Coming, The Russians are Coming.*'
'I didn't know it was from a film. I just wrote what I heard in your music.'
'Well, you must see this film. I'll take you down to the Directors Guild Theatre and you'll see.'
So we went to the theatre, and I was amazed when I saw the love scene played out on the screen. There was the shining sea, the seashells, the young Russian kissing the hollow of the girl's hand . . . Funny how these things happen.

We loved the shining sea
He gathered sea shells there for me
His hands, his strong, brown hands . . .

We'd sit there on the sand
He'd kiss the hollow of my hand
His kiss . . . I miss his kiss . . .

I hear the grey gulls cry
I see them dip their wings
I feel the pounding surf
And other things . . .

I can't believe he's gone
I think I'll go where he might be
I'll go . . . I need him so
I need our shining sea.

Johnny wrote some superb arrangements for my album *Mirrors*: 'I Remember', 'Say It', which is like glass, and there are some beautiful deep dark colours in 'Little White Ship'. One section with the bass clarinet is so beautiful: 'To places dark and deep . . . where you can fall asleep . . . and *dream* . . .'

Johnny's music is like not just a bed of strings, but an ocean of strings, mostly calm, and the moving progressions under the water show what a craftsman he is. His music floats. So it was not surprising that I wanted an arrangement from Johnny in *Peg*.

It's hard to think of the music business without Gordon Jenkins. He could make such beautiful broad brush strokes with his arrangements and such clear, strong, lovely compositions, but he left us in June 1986 . . . not long before we heard 'Goodbye' played so much when Benny Goodman died. Gordon wrote 'Goodbye' for Benny's closing theme.

I remember the first arrangements he did for me at Decca. It was spring, and I was in love with actor Robert Mazurvy. I was all excited because after the date we were going to the Drake Hotel to hear Cy Walter's piano for the first of many times. We would drink Piper Heidseck champagne and watch the captain make Steak Diane and tiny, thin julienne French fried-zucchini . . . but when I saw Gordon and that enormous orchestra, I forgot all about that and sang 'I'm Glad There is You' and 'Forgive Me'.

Gordon and I were to work together many times, each one memorable. Remember how he orchestrated 'Lover'? The last time was when we were rehearsing *Peg*. Cy Coleman, Bobby Drivas and I decided to use as many of the top arrangers as we could think of to do the songs most suited to their particular style of writing. We chose Gordon to write 'Mama'. I didn't know Gordon was so ill. Bev, his beloved wife, said when he called, 'Well, Gordon can't speak, but he most certainly can write. You can speak to him if you wish, and he'll write down the answer.' I thought, 'My God, what an example of courage!' We went through all the details, and he enthusiastically wrote down all the answers we wanted to hear. Later, Bev told me that Gordon couldn't get the song 'Mama' out of his mind.

When the finished arrangement came into the rehearsal hall, we couldn't wait to see what he had written. Cy and Mike Renzi played lines from the arrangement on the piano. We were all in tears before it was finished, so you can imagine how we felt when we finally got to orchestra rehearsal. It was beautiful, so moving.

Every time I sang it I had to steel my emotions. The thought of my Mama, coupled with Gordon Jenkins' inspired writing, was almost more than I could control. I had hoped so desperately that I could record it. When Gordon died, we all lost a major talent. But at least he was able to do *Trilogy* for Frank Sinatra. I lost two good friends then – Joseph 'Sonny' Burke, who produced *Trilogy*, and Gordon.

After *Peg* I picked up the pieces. After all, I had my family, my sister Marianne was with us, too (I didn't know it would be the last year of her life), and I had my new friend Mario Buatta, tall, distinguished and *funny*. He's a brilliant interior designer – years later the government would call on Mario to restore Blair House. One night when I was singing at a cabaret, Mario brought Zip, a chimpanzee, and sat down with him at a ringside table. I couldn't believe my eyes. Surely Mario wouldn't actually bring a monkey to my performance. I decided to treat Zip as a person and he behaved well, listening intently and applauding in all the right places. Then people started disrupting the show, taking pictures of Zip, and I had to say, 'Mario, don't you think it's about his bedtime?' Later in my dressing room I sat down with Zip, but still wouldn't pose for photographers. Zip then leaned over and kissed me, forever winning my heart. I'm fairly easy.

And of course there was Genghis, my little Lhasa Apso. If he'd had hips, he would have had his hands on them. He looked at me out of the corner of his eyes – he slid his pupils along the lower lid until they got to me. Then he slid his eyes back to the oversized teddy bear dressed in a mink coat which Mario Buatta had placed on my bed as a surprise.

Genghis was jealous. He was seventeen years old but he seemed like a healthy little clown, a puppy. He managed to scoot that teddy bear, three times his size, from my king-size bed to the floor and out of the room. He jumped back up on the bed, gave a snuffling snort, curled up and lay down. As I smoothed his fur, I gently remembered what a comfort he'd been to me in New York.

If you're wondering how he got there, this is how it started. Back in Bel Air, I had thought Genghis should travel with me, at least once. So I bought a carrying case – actually a black and white striped Lancôme bag – and had grommets punched in it so he would get plenty of air. Then we got into our daily routine. I would tell him I was taking him to New York, at which point he would lift his little shoulders to let me know he liked the idea. I'd tell him every detail of how he would get in the limo with me and ride to the airport, how we would go through security and into the plane to wait for takeoff. Somewhere in my travelogue lecture I would slip him into the Lancôme bag and zip the zipper, carry him around the house, take him in the elevator, explaining there would be one in the New York suite, as well as a terrace where he could look out and survey New York.

Day after day we rehearsed, until he could hardly wait for the limo. Finally, the day came, and he jumped into the bag. We got into the limo, to the airport, through security. I talked to him all the way. It all went beautifully until we got on the plane and there was a delay, but luckily the stewardess gave me permission to take him out on my lap. He wasn't much of a lap dog, but he was following orders. They brought around *hors d'oeuvres*, and he ate mine, as well as several other passengers'. The plane took off, and he stretched out on his back on my lap. It was a perfect blue-sky day with lots of cumulus nimbus clouds. He lay there for so long, just looking at the clouds. Like Snoopy, I thought, only Genghis was all black with a few silver streaks.

When we arrived in New York, he stayed in the bag until the hotel; then he got out and ran through the lobby to the elevator, rode upstairs with Holly and me and scooted to the terrace I had promised. He let us know in no uncertain terms how happy he was to be there.

He made friends . . . Foobar was a dog who lived at the River Tower on East Fifty-Fourth, and Genghis loved Foobar. Also the doormen Louis and Luciano, the bellman Jamie, the concierge Trebor – everyone he met, including my wardrobe woman, who at first said, 'I don't walk any dem dog!' but later was proud to say, 'Genghis *likes* me!' He was the major domo, running the house, and he turned out to be really a New York dog.

Back on the road again. Holly and I went to Japan with The Quintet – Mike, Grady, Jay, Mark, and John. We had another wonderful, successful stay there, but my little blackouts were beginning to worry me. One night after we came back Tony Bennett introduced me to two of my most beloved friends, Elizabeth and Donald Kramer. It was like meeting another sister to meet Elizabeth. And Donald has such a great sense of humour. We began exchanging jokes and we've been fast friends ever since. They introduced me to Julian Wills, who is the head of Arts International, and before I knew it, I was recording a video cassette for that company. We recorded it in Atlantic City at Resorts International. It wasn't easy – I sang for fourteen hours straight – but it certainly was fun.

I also went to London with The Quintet and had one of the most memorable tours I've made there. We travelled to most of the cities in a grand Daimler, but for one engagement in Scotland, our road manager said, 'We'll take a Viscount.' It was a prop plane, not a jet, and had no ramp. The road manager said, 'We could provide a fork-lift.' 'A fork-lift?' This sounded like Australia, where the photographers caught me being lifted by a fork-lift. My guitarist John Chiodini and I couldn't believe our ears.

We began to examine the plane. 'Do you think we can fly this thing?' I asked. John said, 'We can keep it up there with our faith,' and we both laughed. Several minutes out of Glasgow, I looked at John in amazement: the roof was leaking on his head! It took every bit of faith I had, because it was very clear the plane wasn't pressurized. I thought we were flying out in the Twilight Zone, but the trip was relatively uneventful. I said relatively.

We ended the tour with a triumphant turn at the Royal Festival Hall, and then back to the States.

During this time I was having an occasional heart episode followed by an angiogram or an angioplasty, but in between I was feeling fine, so I was open-minded about blazing new trails.

When agent Irvin Arthur mentioned the Ballroom in New York City, I couldn't quite picture what it was – it could have been a place to stop for a one-nighter with a band, or a huge room with a stage at one end and a whirling mirrored ball hanging from the ceiling. Irwin explained: 'They have a *tapas* bar.' I thought he said topless, but we cleared that up right away, because, of course, I would draw the line there! I learned that Felipe Rojas Lombardi, a world-class chef, was in charge of serving gourmet delicacies in the dining area adjacent to the cabaret, or theatre space. Now it all took on a totally different feeling. And they were certainly being fair financially.

After the heart-rending experience of *Peg* I had a sort of unwritten pact with the fantastic musicians who formed The Quintet that we would work together again and again. Our very successful tours meant we were ready to jump into New York City. So with happy hearts John, Grady, Mike, Mark, Jay, sometimes Emil, and I opened at the Ballroom to cheering crowds and glowing reviews. Rolls-Royces and limousines jammed the street and lines formed again. I'll always remember what the critic John Wilson wrote, 'She looked like a hip angel and she sang like one.'

Greg Dawson, one of the owners of the Ballroom, became a good friend, as did Felipe, Scott, and all the waiters, especially one named Michael, who took great pains serving me Felipe's delicious salmon cooked on mesquite. Then the time came to sadly say goodbye to all our new friends, I had more tests taken, and then went on to an engagement in New Orleans.

New Orleans has always been a favoured place for me, but I wouldn't have dreamed it would almost be my last appearance. We arrived at the Fairmont, once the Roosevelt Hotel, and were greeted by my dear friend Marilyn Barnett (who works as public-relations director at the Hilton Hotel and fairly exudes the charm of New Orleans) and Oliver, the maître d' I remembered from the past.

It felt good to be back and we opened to a generous audience.

We were also excited because we had been invited to a state dinner at the White House at the close of the New Orleans engagement. We were to perform for President and Mrs Reagan, the Prime Minister of the Republic of Singapore and Mrs Lee, and other dignitaries . . .

It was a beautiful October morning, sun shining, a blue-sky day. But inside the New Orleans Fairmont, in Suite 579, it was not so sunny. I needed help. I called Toni Chandler, my assistant: 'Toni, Toni, please come in; I'm having trouble with my heart. Get the nitro.' I dropped the phone. Toni came running from her room. 'What can I get for you? Here's the nitro! The heart box?'

'Yes, call Dr McEachens.' Thank God I could call him like that. I put the pacer-tracer over my heart. There was something wrong all right. The number was ringing. 'Hello, Peggy?' Dr McEachens' quiet, comforting voice. 'Let me hear it,' he said. I turned it on. After seconds, he said, 'Yes, you're in fibrillation. You'd better call the paramedics right away.'

Toni called Marilyn Barnett, who immediately got Dr Tom Oelsener at the Touro Infirmary.

I had felt more than a little concern the night before, and, after conferring with Oliver, the maître d' of the Blue Room, had decided to cancel the second show. That was something major for me, something I *never* did, but, because we were going to the White House, I thought it best to pay attention to the pain and irregularity of my heart. With some rest, I'd be all right, I'd thought. Nothing was going to keep me from the White House.

The ambulance men came so fast. They quietly and efficiently put me on the stretcher, listened with stethoscope, applied blood-pressure cuff, conferred on the telephone, then down the hall, into the ambulance, light whirling, no siren. Toni slid into the front seat with the driver. She said later I was so calm, she didn't realize how serious it was.

Riding through the streets of New Orleans, looking out the back door of the ambulance in the bright morning light, wondering, wondering. It struck me how different this was than riding along on a float during Mardi Gras. I was a little hazy by that time. We arrived at the hospital and they were bundling me around on gurneys; it seemed as though everyone was running in and out with bottles and needles and tapes and tubes.

My friend Marilyn arrived. She must have been the one to call the White House and notify them that I was going into surgery.

My daughter and my granddaughter, Nicki and Holly, flew down, arriving just about two hours before the surgery. Dr Luke Glancy did an angiogram and, by the minute, it was looking more and more urgent that we get things under way.

I remember Dr Charles Pearce, leading a group of doctors, coming in and saying, 'Don't worry, honey, we're going to take care of you.' Diabetes isn't the best thing to have when you're going into surgery. They had the IV drips going and I did wonder if they were giving me glucose, but when things are that bad, you kind of lie back and know that God is working through every one of those wonderful, dedicated people. At least, that's what I did, in my lucid moments.

I was just lying there like a rag doll, full of pain, when Nicki and Holly came in. Nicki kissed me. 'Hello, Mama. I love you, we're with you.' Holly said, 'I love you, Mama Peggy, we'll be praying.' The nurse came to my bed to remove my nail polish and Holly had to chuckle: I didn't want it removed and said, 'Just take it from one finger – leave it on, and please let me keep my eyelashes. You're not going to be operating on my eyes. My glasses! Where are my glasses?'

The nurse patiently talked me into the polish remover and out of the glasses.

'Well, I guess we're ready,' I heard someone say.

Everyone came running alongside the gurney, blowing kisses. I had no sense of fear, just fatigue – and love. The clock was running . . .

I don't remember being in intensive care, don't know how long. There was a blur here and there, but even that could have been a dream.

I just barely awakened to see the flowers. The flowers!

'Peggy, can you see these flowers? They're from President and Mrs Reagan.' My eyes tried to focus. Why don't I remember? . . . I must have made it to the White House, and it must have been a success! Someone read me the telegram they had sent.

Peggy,
Nancy and I are very sorry about your hospitalization. Our prayers are with you and we hope to hear news of your progress soon.

Everyone missed you at the state dinner last night and all ex-
pressed their concern. Please take care and God Bless You.
Ronald Reagan

I thought, 'The President of the United States and Nancy! How did
I ever get here from North Dakota?'

I floated around in my thoughts, then, 'Peggy. Peggy. Can you
wake up just a bit and help us?'

'Hmmm? Oh, I, yes. Lil? Is that you?' Lil Samardzija, the head
of nursing, had a wonderful manner. I went in and out again.

Michael was a male nurse working in the Coronary Care Unit.
Young, tall, handsome and very caring, he was so sensitive he could
almost read my mind, and before I could ask what he was doing in
my room, he had put me at ease. He was a total professional. When
they moved me, I missed him.

I kept hearing about the hurricane we were having in New Orleans
and how in Bures, Louisiana, a tidal wave had washed all the coffins
up out of the cemetery; my mind wandered off to the heat and the
cold we had so many years ago in Wimbledon, and to old Hank
Schultz, the town's alcoholic drayman. I used to feel so sorry for
him. I would drag him from the depot platform into the warm
waiting room so he wouldn't freeze. We became friends.

Once Hank let me ride in the dray wagon. He wanted to get the
horses fed and watered, so he took me to the barn. He unhitched
the horses and took them into their stalls. The barn was warm and
had a mixture of smells – hay mostly and horse and a bit of a manure
smell, but it was clean. Old Hank kept it as nice as you could ask
for, and the horses, you could tell they loved him. They kind of
nudged him and stood there easing off one foot and then another
as they watched him get the hay and the oats. I was fascinated by
all of it . . . Hank always looked like his clothes were way too big
for him. I guess he liked them loose like that, but it all added to his
tramp-like air. He showed a gentle authority with the horses,
though, and kind of a wistful friendliness with me. He was lonely,
no doubt about that.

> There was old Hank Schultz
> Chewin' on a plug . . .
> And in between, he'd take a swig
> From his jug . . .

175

Tobacco juice ran down his beard . . .
What a sad old man – sad and weird.
It was five in the morning when I heard that shot
I was freezing pumping water . . .
Should I run or not?
I knew it was a gun
Knew that something was dead . . .
Hank stumbled in the door
And sobbing he said . . .
'Come with me, kid.
Something's terrible wrong'
So I ran home with him
He was cryin' all along
She was lying in the bed
With a shot through the heart
And old Hank Schultz just fell apart.
Gun fell from her hand
And landed in the drawer
She was staring straight up
And she wasn't anymore . . .
                  People talked . . .
People said 'He must have shot her'
But I knew better . . .
He'd have stopped her if he could
I knew he wouldn't let her . . .
                  Kill herself . . .
                  Poor old Schultz . . .

Sometimes life is sadder than death. Hank was lonelier than ever once she was gone. Even if she was sick, he had somebody to care. And now the whole town turned away from him. They didn't like the way he shuffled around with the aroma of whiskey and chewing tobacco, but more than that, they all thought he killed her.

I'd swear on a stack of Bibles, he didn't. How could he be so kind to those horses? After that, he probably just drank himself away.

Dr James Conway was standing in the doorway. 'Hello, Miss Lee.'
'I don't wish to see you today,' I said to his indistinct form.

'Well,' he said, 'I'd like to examine you.'

He didn't know quite what to say when I responded, 'Why don't you come back tomorrow?' I didn't know he was a specialist in infectious diseases and intensive care, and I just felt so tired.

'I believe I'd better see you today,' he said, and proceeded to examine me.

I thought I was being charming: 'Only yesterday we had a birthday party for my friend Mario Buatta. He at least was dressed for the occasion. He was wearing a cap with a dog sitting on his head. We had dinner sent in from Commanders . . .'

But Dr Conway wasn't interested in all that. I know he didn't want to give the diagnosis he found. It was a staph infection, plus another name I've never heard before or since. So, back to the operating room we went to reopen the incision they had made for the double bypass surgery. His orders were to leave it open for six weeks and there began some *really* intensive care. Nurses Wanda Grimes, Joy and Ilene Shaw started working around the clock, and I mean *they worked*. More flowers came, messages poured in, and they bolstered my spirits.

I discovered Dr Conway had a marvellous sense of humour. He told me how Dr Pearce went to a charity ball for the SPCA, adopted a dog, took it for a walk and broke his leg trying to avoid the puddles left by the hurricane. The dog was so grateful to be adopted, he immediately became Dr Pearce's guard dog and wouldn't let anyone help him. As soon as we could we laughed at all this turn of events. That helped.

Dr Conway was in every day and I'm sure his diligence must have saved me during this last crisis. I could hear the organs in my body doing what they do . . . the lungs sounded like wet wax paper.

Talk of *debridements* was followed by several trips to the operating room. (If tissue begins to heal prematurely around an open wound, they put you to sleep and snip if off.) All of this gave me time to think of what a wonderful mechanism the human body is.

I've been down before many times, even had the death experience, but never so far down as the Touro Infirmary in New Orleans. The doctors all said, 'You've been to hell and back,' and I must admit it was an extraordinary experience, needing every bit of the love that poured into that hospital to pull me back over the edge. Every prayer that was said, every card or letter that was written, every telephone call or telegram or flower or thought, every bit of dedication by the doctors, nurses and technicians, every last soul.

Frank Sinatra called many, many times. I was able to speak to him sometimes, and he gave me strength and kept urging me on to get well: 'We've got to get you home, baby.'

Then, finally, the time came to be released. On the day I left Touro all of those people in that hospital who worked so hard to ensure my recovery were lined up along the route my wheelchair would take. It was time to return to California, to St John's and my own cardiologist, Dr James McEachens and Dr Paris.

Frank Sinatra had arranged for a private plane to fly me, my nurse Wanda Grimes, my assistant Toni, and my daughter Nicki back to the West Coast.

Flying home. Next stop Santa Monica and St John's. ETA: On time. Courtesy of my friend, Frank Sinatra.

Of course, life didn't end right there. In a way it was more like the beginning of a new life.

When I recovered I immediately let everyone know I was ready to go again and began booking tours. Barbara Voltaire and I planned my wardrobe and she began making beautiful gowns, evening coats, and suits. It was so much fun getting all the musicians back into rehearsing. John Chiodini and I started writing. I didn't return to the Ballroom just then because as the old saying goes, you have to crawl before you can walk and the Ballroom schedule was a little too much for me to handle that soon. Of course, I had to have my doctors' approval, and they felt something on the West Coast would be more in line. So we opened in the Westwood Playhouse in Los Angeles and the audience gave me a beautiful reception. There were flowers and great excitement; everyone seemed genuinely happy that I had made it through the surgery.

Then sorrow came again. My beloved sister, Marianne, had been ill for a long time and finally she left us. Her children, Lee, Lynn, and Merrilee, and Nicki and I were holding her hand as she slipped away. I've never known a finer human being. I thought of how she would have wanted me to carry on, how she would buoy me up with her gentle loving spirit. Her daughter, Merrilee, has a lot of her mother's qualities.

But life is good and I'm thinking of going to a little bit of everywhere, including maybe China or Russia and certainly France, Germany,

Italy and Spain! It would be great to go to Japan again. I'm just so grateful to be here, to be alive – still curious, still loving. Of course, I have some moments of getting annoyed about stupid little things, but I'm working on it. Meanwhile, I go on my same philisophical jaunts. Right now I'm reading *Letters of the Scattered Brotherhood*. Open it to nearly every page and your need will be helped.

I've played some awfully exciting places and will continue to do so long as life will let me. Gino Empry, Canada's public-relations guru, still gets me up to Canada and I love it. Recently I had a marvellous time entertaining the National Ballet of Canada here in my home – the dancers, the members of the orchestra, some of whom have played for me in Canada, the entrepreneurs and members of the press. It was an honour to meet the charming consul general and his lovely wife. Makes me think I can't wait to get back to Toronto, where I seem to play every year, then dip down to New York City and play the Ballroom for an interesting and exciting time. I've enjoyed Atlantic City a couple of times and even played Caesars at Las Vegas and Atlantic City with the beloved George Burns.

Last time I did so I slipped on the steel plate on the stage at Caesars and fractured my pelvis, to say nothing of how I bruised my tailbone, which wasn't too nice. It happened the last time I worked with George Burns there. Clay, in the lighting booth, thought I'd had a heart attack and died. The audience had hardly begun their evening, so I said, 'Bring me a chair and put me out by the piano.' George stood in the wings while I sang. Nobody could figure how I was sitting there with a broken pelvis. Neither, I assure you, could I. I did the whole show sitting on one hip. There was a ruffle in the audience as the stretcher-bearers came through, and the minute the curtain went down I was placed on it and an ambulance was waiting. As I went by, George took that cigar out of his mouth and said, 'You're a brave girl, Peg.' Thanks, George. I love you. I've known him since the time when Gracie was alive.

The episode at Caesars changed the balance of my walking, but it's become a game of goals to get back together on my feet. The wheelchair has been a necessary aid, and the walker was help too. I got so good at the walker, I bought a stationary bicycle and proceeded to reinjure myself. Then, trying to walk around the pool, I irritated my toes until they became infected and that sent me to the hospital more than once. All of this is not meant to be a downer.

I've been learning discipline, gaining a little wisdom from books like *The Life and Teachings of the Masters of the Far East*. I've been reading those books for twenty-five years.

I had done a painting for the Franklin Mint through Dick Hodgsons and was delighted when he told me that the American Beauty Rose Society was going to name a rose after me. Some time after that I received forty-eight Peggy Lee rose bushes. They had giant root structures and had to be soaked in every bathtub in the house before planting. I put them out in the garden, where I already had quite a collection of rose bushes – Abe Lincoln, Helen Traubel, Bing Crosby, Peace, Mon Cherie, Sterling and Royal Highness. When the Peggy Lee bloomed, it was extraordinary – seven-by-eight inches in diameter, big cabbage roses they are. The buds are peach coloured and have delicate violet veining running from the centre of the rose. There are also shades of yellow in with the peach and pink. Gradually, as it opens, its delicate perfume is released in the air throughout the garden. It is the most beautiful rose I have ever seen.

I'm not sure I'll be performing standing anymore, but I know I'll be walking on and off stage. You can bet on it! I plan to do another turn or two at the Pasadena Playhouse or some other theatres, and if the body is a little bit reluctant, I *know* the spirit is willing. I plan to be without diabetes and without my glasses, among some other things I don't need, but I *do* need you, and if you like this book I hope to write at least one more – and to sing with those fantastic musicians I love so much. Two or three albums will be coming out, and there're still lots of songs to write and sing. I've started the Peggy Lee Scholarship Fund through the Women's International Centre (with Gloria Lane, the founder) for musicians and singers. I'm trying to give back as much as I can to dear life. I want to be more active in The Songwriters' Guild and ASCAP and the arts in general.

By the way, Frank Sinatra and I did do the cancer benefit we had talked about while I was in St John's. Then I joined Frank and Sammy Davis Jr at Radio City Music Hall for a stunning evening for Sloan-Kettering. And not to forget Rosemary and Danny Thomas' St Jude.

It's a wonderful life.

Index

INDEX

INDEX

INDEX